CINZIA RANDAZZO

THE HEURISTIC ASPECTS OF THE FUNCTION AND OF THE IDENTITY OF THE PNEUMA IN THE FATHERS OF THE CHURCH (I-IV SEC. D.C.)

Youcanprint Self-Publishing

Title The heuristic aspects of the function and of the identity of the pneuma in the Fathers of the church (I-IV sec. d.C.)

ISBN: 978-88-93065-25-2

Youcanprint Self-Publishing
Via Roma, 73 – 73039 Tricase (LE) – Italy
www.youcanprint.it
info@youcanprint.it
Facebook: facebook.com/youcanprint.it
Twitter: twitter.com/youcanprintit.

Preface

This texts explores a topic, which remains understudied and yet it is of extreme importance and actuality - how the early Fathers saw the identity of the Holy Spirit. It concurs with the modern interest in Pneumatology, which for a long period remained in the shadow of the Trinitarian and Christological doctrines. The study proves the insight of the modern scholarship that the early Christianity before its coming under the umbrella of the Roman Empire enjoyed more diversity in its life and doctrine than afterwards. The early Fathers' views on the role of the Spirit in the life of God and of the world were not an exception from this rule. The study is highly informative and presents its subject in a systematic and yet entertaining way. It is a comprehensive introduction to the early Christian Pneumatology for everyone who wants to know more about it.

Kiev, 8-4-2015   Cyril HOVORUN

Teacher and researcher

in the seminary of theology

In this work, Cinzia Randazzo investigates the function and the identity of the Holy Spirit in the Church Fathers between the first and fourth centuries of our era. The Apostolic Fathers remained close to the figure of the Holy Spirit as it appears in the New and the Old Testament. The Apologists broadened the perspective by enquiring into the relations of the Holy Spirit with the Father and the Son, and by making it the source of prophetic inspiration. With Irenaeus, Origen, Tertullian, and Cyprian, the fight against heresies concerning its place and role within the Trinity became dominant; we find this tendency in the Cappadocian Fathers. In Clement of Alexandria, the importance of the Holy Spirit takes on increased importance, thanks to numerous borrowings from various philosophical tendencies.

Here is a striking example. What distinguishes the Christian doctrine of the Holy Spirit from Plato's is the divine breath received on the occasion of creation, which makes intellect (*nous*) enter man's very constitution. Its coming is greeted as a divine favor (*theía moíra*):

Hence the Pythagoreans say that intellect (*noûs*)

comes to man by <u>divine dispensation</u> (*theíai moírai*), as <u>Plato</u> and Aristotle avow; but we assert that the <u>Holy Spirit</u> (*ágion pneûma*) inspires him who has <u>believed</u>. The Platonists hold that intellect is an effluence of divine dispensation in the <u>soul</u> (*noûn en psukhêi theías moíras apórroian hupárkhonta*), and they place the <u>soul</u> in the body. For it is expressly said by Joel, one of the twelve <u>prophets</u>: «And it shall come to pass after these things, I will pour out of My Spirit on all flesh, and your sons and your daughters shall prophesy.» (Joel 3, 1) But it is not as a portion of <u>God</u> (*méros theoû*) that the Spirit (*pneûma*) is in each of us. But how this dispensation takes place, and what the <u>Holy Spirit</u> is, shall be shown by us in the books on <u>prophecy</u>, and in those on the <u>soul</u>. But incredulity is <u>good</u> at concealing the depths of <u>knowledge</u>, according to Heraclitus; for incredulity escapes from <u>ignorance</u>. (*Stromata* V 88, 1-2.)

A comparison with *Stromata* VI 134, 2 shows that *Genesis* 2, 7 applies to the intellect that comes to man by divine favor (= 8th element of the decad) and that the Spirit of *Joël* 3, 1 (V 88, 3), corresponds to "the Holy Spirit breathed into he who has faith" (V 88, 2), that is, to the 10th element of the decade of VI, 134, 2: "the characteristic property of the Holy Spirit, which is added by virtue of faith". This presence, added to the human compound, is reserved for prophets and those who receive baptism, as is shown by the symbolic explanation given in *Stromata* IV, 116, 2 (cf. *Prophetic eclogues*, 13, 9, among others).

A comparison with *Stromata* VI 134, 2 shows that *Genesis* 2, 7 applies to the intellect that comes to man by divine favor (= 8th element of the decad), and that the Spirit of *Joël* 3, 1 (V 88, 3) corresponds to "the Holy Spirit breathed into he who has faith" (V 88, 2), that is, to the 10th element of the decade of *Stromata* VI, 134, 2: "the characteristic property of the Holy Spirit, which is added by virtue of faith". This presence, added to the human compound, is reserved for prophets and those who receive baptism, as is shown by the symbolic explanation given in *Stromata* IV, 116, 2.

It should be noted, moreover, that the image of an outpouring (*apórroia*) to designate the intellect (*nous*) is also present in Middle Platonism. One should also note that in Clement's time, Pythagoreanism and Platonism

6

went hand-in-hand; this is why a similar doctrine is attributed to the Pythagoreans. For Aristotle, one might think of the *Nicomachean Ethics*. The last sentence of the citation is probably directed against the Stoics. Indeed, at the foundation of Stoic cosmology one finds the following two principles. One can only undergo effects: this is matter, bereft of all determination, all motion and all initiative. The other has the ability to act and brings form, quality, and motion to matter in inanimate objects, plants, animals and men. This second principle is "reason" (*lógos*) which is a fiery breath, the omnipresent *pneûma*.

Paris,8-4-2015

Luc BRISSON

CNRS -Paris

Introduction

The present study intends to delineate, for highest heads, the most meaningful lines of the theology of the Spirit in the Fathers. To reach such purpose, in a first moment, we will try to extract by the sources the affirmations connected to the concept of the Spirit in the Fathers, while, in a second moment, to clarify the thought of the Fathers with respect to the proposed theme, we will use, if possible, recent commentaries and monographs. Consequently the Christian authors will be quoted by the most recent and reliable editions, indicated to the relative references.

This search however will be conducted within a well precise historical period: it's about the arc of time that goes from the I century d.C. to the IV century d.C., period that is extended from the epoch of the apostolic Fathers until the fathers Cappadocian included. Our search, limitedly to such period of time, is divided in five paragraphs.

In a first paragraph we will try to point out the fundamental characteristics of the theology of the Spirit in the apostolic Fathers. Subsequently in a second paragraph we will underline the essential characteristics of the Spirit in the Fathers apologists, pointing out the continuity or the difference with the apostolic Fathers. Subsequently in a third paragraph it will be shown, in the field of the controversy against the heretics, the fundamental properties of the Spirit. In the IV paragraph we will try to give a panorama of the reflections that Clement of Alexandria and Origen to Alexandria and Tertullian and Ciyprian to Carthage have expressed above all on the divine reality of the Spirit. Finally in the fifth and last paragraph it will emerge by the thought of the Fathers Cappadocian the fundamental notions of the doctrine of the Spirit. From this whole study it is possible show the convergences or the divergences of ideas of the Spirit among a father to another and above all the doctrinal developments that result of it. With regard to the dogmatic development of the category of the Spirit, that is object of our study, and, bearing in mind the words of the *Dei Verbum* 8, according to which the Spirit Holy guides the believers to a knowledge more deepened of the revealed datum, it is opportune to underline that in a future perspective it will can subsequently be specified and deepened the formulas of the Spirit that the Fathers have used within the first four centuries. On the base of such considerations therefore we wish ourselves that this search be the opportune occasion to reach a deeper and adequate knowledge of the thought of the Fathers of the Church on the third person of the Spirit, aware nevertheless that in the thought of the Fathers are contained inexhaustible wealths concerning the Spirit, that have not been entirely still explained.

INDEX

Preface

Introduction

1. THE HEURISTIC ASPECTS OF THE FUNCTION AND OF THE IDENTITY OF THE SPIRIT IN THE APOSTOLIC FATHERS

1.1. *The previous existence of the Spirit*

Before penetrating in this search, we believe opportune to remember that for Apostolic Fathers it's intended the Fathers lived within the end of the first century until the first half of the second century; period in which it's shown an abundant literary production, where it's pointed out the life of faith of the first communities that believed in God, in Jesus Christus and in the Spirit Holy and therefore a first and simple organization of the revealed datum. To such intention J.P. MARTIN writes in fact:

> When the first christians said to believe in the Spirit Holy, the object of this faith was not that God has the Spirit, not even that the Spirit is God, because the tautologies are never object of faith. It's affirmed instead a historical fact, that is to say the faith in the manifestation of God in the community of

the christians.[1]

It rises spontaneous to this point the question: what the Apostolic Fathers affirm on the datum revealed of the Spirit Holy? This is the object of our search.

Before other all Fathers Hermas, who is an apostolic Father of the first half of the second century, tells us, in the *Shepherd,* that the Spirit Holy existed before the creation and it was also creator: "*God made to live in the flesh that he wanted the Spirit Holy who existed before the creation and who did every creature*".[2] Hermas refers to Giovanni, according to whom the Spirit Holy has existed before all the things because he comes from the sky (Gv 3,3-9.15,26). The Spirit in Hermas also has a connotation christological, because it's also

---

1 J.P. MARTIN, *Il rapporto tra Pneuma ed Ecclesia nella letteratura dei primi secoli cristiani,* in "Augustinianum"20 (1980), p. 483. Per il periodo   storico dei Padri Apologisti cfr. C. BOSIO-E. DAL COVOLO-M. MARITANO, *Introduzione ai Padri della chiesa, sec. I-II,* vol. I, Torino 1990; C. MORESCHINI-E. NORELLI, *Storia della letteratura cristiana antica greca e latina*, vol. I, Morcelliana, Brescia 1996; J. QUASTEN, *Patrologia,* vol. I, Casale 1983.

2 ERMA, *Pastore. Similitudini* V,6,5. Ed. crit. F. XAVER FUNK-K. BIHLMEYER-M. WHITTAKER, *Die Apostolischen Väter. Griechisch-deutsche Parallelausgabe,* Tübingen 1992, p. 446. Trad. di A. QUACQUARELLI, *I Padri Apostolici*, Roma 1998, p. 300.

denominated son of God: "*The Spirit is the son of God*".[3] Since previously Hermas had affirmed that "the Spirit is the son of God", for Hermas the Spirit Holy comes to coincide with the Son of God, preexisting together with the Father.

1.1.1. The function of the Spirit in the old Testament: the Spirit Holy font of prophetic inspiration

The Spirit Holy preexisting has wanted to make known in advance the divine plan of the salvation, inspiring not only the prophets but also the other books of the old Testament. Clement of Rome in fact affirms that, through the prophet Ezekiel, the Spirit Holy has spoken of the repentance:

> The ministers of the grace of God spoke of the repentance through the Spirit Holy. Also the Lord of all the things talked of the repentance together with the oath: "I live – says the Lord - and I don't want the death of

---

3 ERMA, *Pastore. Similitudini* IX,1,1. Ed. crit. F. XAVER FUNK-K. BIHLMEYER-M. WHITTAKER, *Die Apostolischen Väter. Griechisch-deutsche Parallelausgabe,* p. 484. Trad. di A QUACQUARELLI, *I Padri Apostolici,* p. 316

the sinner, on the contrary his conversion (Ez 33,11).[4]

For Clement of Rome always the Spirit Holy is the protagonist of the inspiration of the old Testament and, for this motive, everything is conformed to truth:

you be full of emulation and of zeal in the
things that concern the salvation. You be bent
on the Sacred Writings, the true, given by the
Spirit Holy. You be convinced that nothing of
unfair and of forgery is written in them.[5]

Also for the pseudo-Barnabas in 12,2 the Spirit Holy is the spokesman of the will of salvation of God and for this it tells Moses to hold the hands lifted in sign of the cross, to motive of which the Israelis were saved:

The Spirit tells to the heart of Moses to make
a figure of cross and of the one who would

---

4 CLEMENTE ROMANO, *Lettera ai Corinti* 8,1-2. Ed. crit. F. XAVER FUNK- K. BIHLMEYER-M. WHITTAKER, *Die Apostolischen Väter. Griechisch-deutsche Parallelausgabe*, p. 88. Trad. di A. QUACQUARELLI, *I Padri Apostolici*, p. 54.

5 CLEMENTE ROMANO, *Lettera ai Corinti* 45,1-3. Ed. crit. F. XAVER FUNK-K. BIHLMEYER-M. WHITTAKER, *Die Apostolischen Väter. Griechisch- deutsche Parallelausgabe*, p. 128. Trad. di A. QUACQUARELLI, *I Padri Apostolici*, Roma 1998, p. 300.

have had to suffer because – say- if they won't believe in him they will be attacked forever. Moses set to the center of the fray the weapons one on the other, and, set himself more up of all the men, stretched the hands, and in this manner Israel returned to win. Then, when it lowered them, they returned to be killed: Because? Because they knew that it cannot be saved if don't hope in him.[6]

1.1.2. The identity of the function of the Spirit in relationship to Christ

a. The identity christological of the Spirit

The Spirit Holy preexisting, who has inspired the prophets, has been also the one who has realized the incarnation. Hermas, to such regard, declares that the Spirit embodies himself; that same Spirit who in *Similitudes* 9,1,1 is also denominated son of God:

6 CLEMENTE ROMANO, *Lettera ai Corinti* 45,1-3. Ed. crit. F. XAVER FUNK-K. BIHLMEYER-M. WHITTAKER, *Die Apostolischen Väter. Griechisch- deutsche Parallelausgabe,* p. 128. Trad. di A. QUACQUARELLI, *I Padri Apostolici,* Roma 1998, p. 300.

God made to live in the flesh that he wanted the Spirit Holy who pre-existed and who did every creature. This flesh, where taken abode the Spirit Holy, served well the Spirit walking in the holiness and in the chastity, and didn't contaminate him in nothing.[7]

To such intention it seems pertinent the consideration of R. Joly, for whom the Spirit Holy comes to be the divine nature of Christ, ever since the same Hermas in *Similitudes* IX,12,2 affirms that the Son of God already existed still before the creation of the world:

> Pour Hermas, c'est le Saint Esprit qui s'est incarné en Jesus. On a voulu, pour sauver l'orthodoxie d'Hermas, comprendre par Saint-Esprit la nature divine du Christ. Cf. 89,2 où c'est le Fils de Dieu qui est antérieur à toute créature.[8]

In the 2*Epistle* of Clement *to the Corinthians* 9,5 the

---

7 ERMA, *Pastore. Similitudini* V,6,5. Ed. crit. F. XAVER FUNK-K. BIHLMEYER-M. WHITTAKER, *Die Apostolischen Väter. Griechisch-deutsche Parallelausgabe*, p. 446. Trad. di A. QUACQUARELLI, *I Padri Apostolici*, p. 300.
8 R. JOLY (a cura di), *Hermas, Le Pasteur,* Paris 1958, p. 239 n. 3.

platonic inheritance is evident; the flesh of Christ, where the church appears, is in fact copy of the Spirit (preexisting Christ). Inheritance that the author same confirms in 14,3:

> The Church that is spiritual appeared in the flesh of Christ, showing to us that who safeguards her in the flesh and doesn't contaminate her it will receive her in the Spirit Holy. This flesh is image of the Spirit. Nobody who destroys the copy will can change the original one.[9]

Also W. Rordorf, with regard to the 2*Epistle* of Clement *to the Corinthians* 9,5 affirms that

> in effects, doesn't speak of two sons, but of the eternal nature of the only Son who is spiritual; in the incarnation, this spiritual nature is united to that one carnal.[10]

---

9 Ed. crit. F. XAVER FUNK-K. BIHLMEYER-M. WHITTAKER, *Die Apostolischen Väter. Griechisch-deutsche Parallelausgabe,* pp. 166-168. Trad. di A. QUACQUARELLI, *I Padri Apostolici,* p. 230.
10 W. RORDORF, *"Qui natus est de Spiritu sancto et Maria Virgine"*, in "Augustinianum"20 (1980), p. 555.

Subsequently Ignatius exhorts the community to live in harmony and in unity with the other christian communities, only if they possess the spirit of Christ who is the Spirit Holy: " *you is well in the harmony of God possessing the inseparable spirit who is Jesus Christus*".[11] Illuminating it is, to such intention, the affirmation of S. Priest:

> It's observed nevertheless that everything is moved for work of the Spirit, who is everything one with Christ, because it is in his sign that it is strengthened the harmony and the unity of the christians.[12]

b. The Spirit tie of unity between flesh and spirit in Christ

The Spirit, as tie of unity in the flesh and in the spirit of Jesus, is pointed out in the *letter* of Ignatius *to the Magnesians* 1,2:

---

11 IGNAZIO, *Lettera ai Magnesii* 15,1. Ed. crit. F. XAVER FUNK-K. BIHLMEYER - M. WHITTAKER, *Die Apostolischen Väter. Griechisch-deutsche Parallelausgabe,* p. 198. Trad. di A. QUACQUARELLI, *I Padri Apostolici,* p. 114.

12 S. PRETE, *In incorruptibilitate (ἀφθαρσία) Spiritus s. (Mart. Polyc. 14,2)*, in "Augustinianum" 20 (1980), p. 512.

Honoured of a name of a divine shine, in these chains that I bring, I sing to the churchs and I wish them the union in the flesh and in the spirit of Jesus Christus, our eternal life, of the faith and of the charity, which nothing is to prefer, and what is more important "the union" with Jesus and the Father.[13]

Ignatius exhorts once more the community to produce harmony with regard to all what concerns the works of the flesh and of the Spirit, taking to exemplary model the union that exists in the Father, in the Son and in the Spirit:

You try to hold you well firm in the precepts of the Lord and of the apostles because succeeds well you all what you do in the flesh and in the spirit, in the faith and in the charity, in the Son, in the Father and in the Spirit, to the principle and to the end, with

13 Ed. crit. F. XAVER FUNK-K. BIHLMEYER-M. WHITTAKER, *Die Apostolischen Väter. Griechisch-deutsche Parallelausgabe,* p. 192. Trad. di A. QUACQUARELLI *I Padri Apostolici,* p. 109.

your bishop who is very worthy and with the precious spiritual crown of your presbyteries and the deacons according to God. You is subdued to the bishop and the one to the others as Jesus Christus to the Father, in the flesh, and the apostles to Christ and to the Father and to the Spirit, so that the union be carnal and spiritual.[14]

This conception of the Spirit, as it holds united the humanity and the divinity in Christ so it holds united the Christians who form the church, it's found in the most ancient Christian *homily* of the pseudo-Clement:

If we say that the church is the flesh and Christ the Spirit, therefore who violates the flesh violates the Church and won't participate any Spirit who is Christ. To such life and to the incorruptibility this flesh can participate if to her the Spirit Holy is united. Nobody can express and to say what the

---

14 Ps. BARNABA, *Epistola* 1,2. Ed. crit. F. XAVER FUNK-K. BIHLMEYER-M. WHITTAKER, *Die Apostolischen Väter. Griechisch-deutsche Parallelausgabe,* p. 26. Trad. di F.S. BARCELLONA *Epistola di Barnaba*, pp. 78-79.

Lord has prepared for his elected.[15]

Especially in Ignatius the apostle's perspective Paul of the dissension among the flesh, that represents the human principle and the spirit that represents, who represents the soul of the man, is inverted for the fact that both, as affirms S. Priest are placed «*in function of relationship for the unity, as in Mg. 1,2 and 13,1*»".[16] These words recall the desire of the apostle to see in the communities from him established spiritual men, who have received such identity by the strength of the Spirit (1 Cor 3,1.2,6. Ef 6,11-17).

1.2. *The explication of the function of the Spirit in the Church*

1.2.1. The messianic function of the Spirit Holy

We have previously said that the Spirit Holy was the prophetic spirit who announced a future event of salvation, according to the will of God Father. This future event of salvation was the messia who is come on the earth; messia who represents the point of arrival or better

---

15 *Ibidem*

16 S. PRETE, *In incorruptibilitate,* pp. 512-513 n. 16.

the conclusion of the ancient prophecies inspired by the Spirit Holy. In this sense the Spirit Holy becomes the author of the prophecies in messianic perspective. Clement of Rome introduces to us this role of the Spirit Holy, turned to disclose the messianic secret of the royal coming of the Son of God Jesus Christ in the humility, to give to us the salvation:

> Christ is of the humble ones, not whose raises on his flock. The scepter of the majesty of God, the Lord Jesus Christus, didn't come in the din of the boldness and of the pride – and he would have been able it – but in the humility of heart as the Spirit Holy had to say of him: «Lord, who believed in our voice? And the Lord's arm to who was revealed? We announced him to his presence (…) (Is 53,1-12). And again he says: «I am a worm and not a man, infamy of the men and contempt of the people. All those who see me mock me, they speak among the lips and they move the head: he has trusted in the Lord, he frees him, he safes him because he

wants it» (Sal 22,7-9). See, dear, what model there is given! If the Lord is humbled oneself to such point, what will do we who, for his mean, be come under the yoke of his grace?.[17]

1.2.2. The charismas of the Spirit

The Spirit Holy, as divine spirit and therefore preexisting to the world, enriches the christian communities with the charismas. For Clement of Rome one among the so many charismas that the Spirit Holy has emitted in the heart of the men, it is the gift of the stability; gift that had been preannounced by the Spirit in the prophecy of Is 60,17, and it had been transmitted by the Church to those who were designated and elected by the same Spirit to unwind these taskes, that is to say those ones of bishop and of deacon:

---

17 CLEMENTE ROMANO, *Lettera ai Corinti* 16,1-17. Ed. crit. F. XAVER FUNK-K. BIHLMEYER-M. WHITTAKER, *Die Apostolischen Väter. Griechisch- deutsche Parallelausgabe,* pp. 124-126. Trad. di A. QUACQUARELLI, *I Padri Apostolici*, pp. 59-60. Cfr. anche ps. BARNABA, *Epistola* 5,1-14. Ed. crit. F. XAVER FUNK-K. BIHLMEYER-M. WHITTAKER, *Die Apostolischen Väter. Griechisch-deutsche Parallelausgabe,* pp. 34-38.

Received the order and heights of certainty in the resurrection of our Lord Jesus Christus and confident in God's word with the insurance of the Spirit Holy they went to announce that the kingdom of God was about to come. They preached for the countries and the cities and they constituted their novelties, trying them in the spirit, in the bishops and in the deacons of the faithful futures.[18]

Clement continues with to list the numerous gifts that the Spirit Holy has

emitted in the church. Always for Clement the gift of the grace comes from the Spirit Holy who, since unique, brings manifold benefits which the sense of the peace, of the harmony, of the unity, of the goodness, of the joy, of the fortitude and of the perfection

---

18 CLEMENTE ROMANO, *Lettera ai Corinti* 42,3-4. Ed. crit. F. XAVER FUNK-K. BIHLMEYER-M. WHITTAKER, *Die Apostolischen Väter. Griechisch- deutsche Parallelausgabe,* pp. 124-126. Trad. di A. QUACQUARELLI, *I Padri Apostolici*, p. 77.

in the love.[19]

The *Epistle* of Clement is placed in line of continuity with the primitive communities founded by Paul, where, as affirms C. RIGGI,

> the primitive community lived the action of the Spirit through the effusion of sanctifying grace and the extraordinary donation of special charismas (...).[20]

1.2.3. The pneumatas

The immediate effect that the Spirit Holy has produced through the effusion of the charismas it is the reception of the gifts in the soul of the believers. The pseudo- Barnabas therefore rejoyces some fact that the grace of the spiritual gift has taken root in the believers of his community:

> Since the dispositions of God are great and plentiful to your regard, I rejoyce above

---

19 Cfr. CLEMENTE ROMANO, *Lettera ai Corinti* 46,5-7; 50,3;55,3;63,2. Ed. crit. F. XAVER FUNK-K. BIHLMEYER-M. WHITTAKER, *Die Apostolischen Väter. Griechisch-deutsche Parallelausgabe,* pp. 130;134;138;148.

20 C. RIGGI, *Lo Spirito Santo nell'antropologia della I Clementis,* in "Augustinianum"20 (1980), p. 506 n. 13.

every saying for yours blessed and glorious spirits ($\pi\nu\epsilon\hat{\upsilon}\mu\alpha\varsigma\iota\nu$): so much it is rooted in you the grace of the spiritual ($\pi\nu\epsilon\upsilon\mu\alpha\tau\iota\kappa\acute{\eta}$) gift that you have received.[21]

In 4,11 the pseudo-Barnabas makes intend that the man not becomes wise and spiritual for own will, but for the Spirit of God who resides in the heart of the believers:

In fact the Writing says: «woe betide those who is considered wise and it is intelligent to theirs eyes». Let's become spiritual, let's become a perfect temple for God ! However it's possible us, let's apply us to the fear of God and let's fight for observing his commandments to be able to rejoyce in his dispositions.[22]

In 16,10 the pseudo-Barnabas explains in fact that the believer is the spokesman of the word of God, who lives

---

21 Ps. BARNABA, *Epistola* 1,2. Ed. crit. F. XAVER FUNK-K. BIHLMEYER- M. WHITTAKER, *Die Apostolischen Väter. Griechisch-deutsche Parallelausgabe,* p, 26. Trad. di F.S. BARCELLONA *Epistola di Barnaba*, pp. 78-79.

22 Ed. crit. F. XAVER FUNK-K. BIHLMEYER-M. WHITTAKER, *Die Apostolischen Väter. Griechisch-deutsche Parallelausgabe,* p. 34. Trad. di F.S. BARCELLONA, *Epistola di Barnaba,* p. 87.

in him through the gift of the grace:

> in fact who wants to be saved doesn't look at
> the man, but to whom lives and it speaks in
> him, marveling at non the having heard
> never to pronounce with his mouth such
> words and non to have desired never to hear
> them. This is the spiritual temple that is built
> to the Lord.[23]

Insofar, for the pseudo-Barnabas, who listens the believer it listens not his word but that one of God who is replaced in him for work of the Spirit Holy, so that the one who listen to the believer reaches the salvation.

1.2.4. The function anthropological-sanctifier of the Spirit.

We have seen that the Spirit lives in the heart of the believers, because of the effusion of his gifts that have been consequently received by the same believers and lived in the harmony. But it rises spontaneous the

---

23 Ed. crit. F. XAVER FUNK-K. BIHLMEYER-M. WHITTAKER, *Die Apostolischen Väter. Griechisch-deutsche Parallelausgabe,* pp. 66-68. Trad. di F.S. BARCELLONA, *Epistola di Barnaba,* p. 119.

question: which is the role of the Spirit in the man and consequently in the community of the church, because the man reaches the full knowledge of God? Clement of Rome gives us the following answer: as the soldiers perform the commands of their rulers and as the body cannot be without the head and without the feet, in this way every faithful, each according to his grace, is subdued to Christ because from Him he has received all the goods.[24]

From this text we can deduce that the Spirit Holy performs his action of mutual deacony among the brothers and with God and is the one who brings the believers to recognize themselves dependent the one from the others and the one and the others with Christ, as Clement of Rome specifies in 16,17:

> See, dear, what model there is given! If the
> Lord is humbled oneself to such point, what
> will do we who, by his means, be come

---

24 Cfr. *Lettera ai Corinti* 37,1-4.38,1-4. Ed. crit. F. XAVER FUNK-K. BIHLMEYER-M. WHITTAKER, *Die Apostolischen Väter. Griechisch-deutsche Parallelausgabe,* pp. 120.122. Trad. di A. QUACQUARELLI, *I Padri Apostolici,* pp. 74-75.

under the yoke of his grace?.[25]

How Christ, Clement of Rome affirms, has lived in the charity, equally the believers who live in the mutual charity can reach their Father:

> The charity unites us to God: «the charity covers a lot of the sins». The carity all suffers, all bears. Nothing of banal, nothing of proud in the charity. The charity not has schism, the charity not rebel itself, the charity everything fulfils in the harmony. In the charity are perfect all the chosen of God. Without charity nothing is accept to God. In the charity the Lord has taken us to himself. For the charity that it had for us, Jesus Christus our Lord, in the will of God, has given for us his blood, his flesh for our flesh and his soul for our soul.[26]

25 CLEMENTE ROMANO, *Lettera ai Corinzi* 16,17. Ed. crit. F. XAVER FUNK-K. BIHLMEYER-M. WHITTAKER, *Die Apostolischen Väter. Griechisch-deutsche Parallelausgabe,* p. 98. Trad. di A. QUACQUARELLI, *I Padri Apostolici,* p. 60.
26 CLEMENTE ROMANO, *Lettera ai Corinti* 49,5-6. Ed. crit. F. XAVER FUNK-K. BIHLMEYER-M. WHITTAKER, *Die Apostolischen Väter. Griechisch- deutsche Parallelausgabe,* pp. 132-134. Trad. di A. QUACQUARELLI, *I Padri*

Also Ignatius, in his *letter to the Ephesians* 9,1-2, give us the illuminating image of the rope applied to the Spirit Holy. He is the principle of cohesion between the sky and the earth, spirit of communion among the limbs of the believers and Christ, through whom the believers be conducted to God:

> You be stones of the temple of the Father
> prepared for the construction of God Father,
> elevated with the winch of Jesus Christus
> that it is the cross, using as rope the Spirit
> Holy. The faith is your lever and the charity
> the road that conducts you to God.[27]

Then, always for Ignatius of Antioch, the Spirit Holy is the middleman, the one who does by medium between the earth and the sky, because the believers reach the salvation. Without the rope, that is the Spirit Holy, it is impossible to go back to the eternal life from a condition of sin where the man is trapped since the birth. However the Spirit Holy, for the *Shepherd* of Hermas, permits to

Apostolici, pp. 81-82.

27 Ed. crit. F. XAVER FUNK-K. BIHLMEYER-M. WHITTAKER, *Die Apostolischen Väter. Griechisch-deutsche Parallelausgabe,* p. 184. Trad. di A QUACQUARELLI, *I Padri Apostolici,* pp. 102-103

the flesh this process of gone back up and of sanctification, only when this not contaminates the Spirit:

God made live in the flesh that wanted the Spirit Holy who pre-existed and that every creature did. This flesh, where taken abode the Spirit Holy, it served well the Spirit walking in the holiness and in the chastity, and didn't contaminate him in nothing. He choses this flesh to participate some Spirit Holy, because it was behaved worthily and chastely and it had suffered with the Spirit collaborating in every thing and conducting itself with fortitude. To God liked the behavior of this flesh that, having the Spirit Holy, didn't stain itself on the earth. It tooks as advisor the son and the glorious angels because this flesh, having obeyed to the Spirit with satisfaction, it obtained a curtain and didn't seem to have lost the reward of its service. Every flesh found again pure and without stain will receive a reward; in it the

Spirit Holy lived.[28]

1.3. The accomplishment of the function of the
Spirit: the pneumatic gift of the eternal life

By the identity of the church with the flesh and by the identity of Christ with the Spirit, as we have previously seen, it is deduced, always according to the 2*Epistle* of Clement *to the Corinthians* 14,3-5, that who guards the church in the flesh without to contaminate it, since the flesh is image of the Spirit Holy, it will participate in the life of the Spirit and therefore in the incorruptibility of the divine life. Instead who contaminates the flesh, it contaminates the church, why the flesh can participate in the incorruptible life of the single Spirit if it's united to the Spirit:

> the church that is spiritual appeared in the flesh of Christ, showing to us that who safeguards it in the flesh and doesn't contaminate it will receive it in the Spirit

28 ERMA, *Pastore. Similitudini* 59,6,5-7. Ed. crit. F. XAVER FUNK-K. BIHLMEYER-M. WHITTAKER, *Die Apostolischen Väter. Griechisch-deutsche Parallelausgabe*, p. 446. Trad. di A. QUACQUARELLI, *I Padri Apostolici*, p. 300.

Holy. This flesh is image of the Spirit. Nobody who destroys the copy can change the original one. This means, brothers, let's guard the flesh to participate in the Spirit. If we say that the church is the flesh and Christ the Spirit, therefore who violates the flesh it violates the church and won't participate any Spirit who is Christ. To such life and to the incorruptibility this flesh can participate if to it the Spirit Holy is united .[29]

Polycarp instead sees in the martyrdom the street that brings to the incorruptibility of the Spirit Holy and to the eternal life of the soul and of the body:

I bless you, because you have made me worthy of this day and of this time to take part in the number of the martyrs to the chalice of your Christ for the resurrection of the eternal life of the soul and of the body in the incorruptibility of the Spirit Holy.[30]

29 Ed. crit. F. XAVER FUNK-K. BIHLMEYER-M. WHITTAKER, *Die Apostolischen Väter. Griechisch-deutsche Parallelausgabe,* pp. 166-168. Trad. di A. QUACQUARELLI, *I Padri Apostolici*, p. 230.
30 *Martirio di Policarpo* 14,2. Ed. crit. F. XAVER FUNK-K.

2. THE HEURISTIC ASPECTS OF THE FUNCTION AND OF THE IDENTITY OF THE SPIRIT IN THE FATHERS APOLOGISTS

First of all for Fathers Apologists we intend the Fathers of the II century.[31] Unlike the apostolic Fathers, the apologists were compared with the surrounding world and that is to say with the paganism then ruling, comparison not always easy, often animated by persecutions. The purpose of the apologists was not much that one to convince the pagans to adhere to the christian faith, as that one to make them clear the authenticity of the message and its high moral value. The Father apologists, inserted in the field cultural pagan and from this deriving ones and full of culture, in the presenting the christian message, they used some cultural tools in them possession, to suitably be understood by the polytheistical world and religious, which the greek-roman was in all his territorial extension. Under this aspect there is to say that the native kerigma, also

---

BIHLMEYER-M. WHITTAKER, *Die Apostolischen Väter. Griechisch-deutsche Parallelausgabe,* pp. 274-276. Trad. di A. QUACQUARELLI, *I Padri Apostolici*, p. 168.

31 Cfr. C. BOSIO-E. DAL COVOLO-M. MARITANO, *Introduzione*, vol. I, pp. 155-160.

acquiring terms and formal conceptions of type ellenistic, it never betrayed the relative content of faith, on the contrary the translation of the kerigma in the expressive means proper of greek culture favored a deeper understanding of the message on behalf of the pagans. In fact the kerigma, contained in the philosophical categories, has been enriched of new concepts, following the impact of the same kerigma with the most varied existing cultures in such period, with the purpose to present it in clear manner not only to the pagan public, but also in the same church. In such perspective it's developped the apologetical: the church, more than to defend the kerigma, intends to introduce the evangelical message to the cultured pagans of the epoch, using the tools proper of the greek culture to push them to adhere to the christianity. If it is possible therefore to speak of the hellenizzation of the christian announcement, why the datum of the kerigma has been in a certain manner influenced by the greek conceptions, is also possible to speak of the christianization of the hellenism, since will be influenced by the christianity the philosophical currents of the epoch. From such perspective we see, to such intention, which is the role of the Spirit Holy in the Fathers apologists.

2.1. *The function of the Spirit before the creation: the Christ "anointed" by the Spirit of God*

In the 2*Apology* 6,3 Justin affirms that the preexisting logos (Verb) and co-eternal to the Father, before the world was created, is denominated Christ, since has been anointed: "His Son, the only to good right called "Son", the coexistent logos and generated before the creation when to the beginning through him it created and it ordered every thing, it's called Christ, because it has been anointed".[32]

Here Justin evidently refers to the rite of the unction that, for the Hebrews, has the meaning of consecration: in fact in the history of Israel the unction was imparted to the kings, to the prophets and the priests because to them it had been entrusted the office to guide the people of Israel. Justin, associating the unction to Christ, it's placed in line of continuity with the discourse that Pietro did to

---

32 Ed. crit. M. MARCOVICH, *Iustini martyris. Apologiae pro christianis*, p. 145. Trad. di A.R. RACCONE, *Giustino. Le due apologie*, Milano 2004, p. 141.

Cornelio, why God, having consecrated in Spirit Holy Jesus of Nazareth, has conferred him the mission to save all those who were under the power of the demon (At 10,38).

2.2. *The function of the Spirit in the creation: the Spirit Holy transcendent in comparison with the world*

Justin and the other apologists, influenced by the philosophical current middle-platonic,[33] come to the idea that God is absolutely transcendent in comparison with the world. Justin particularly, in the *Dialogue with Trypho*, makes intend that the Spirit is divine as the Son, who has been generated by the Father:

> Let's will give you, friends, - I still said –
> also another testimony taken out by the
> Writings, according to which as beginning
> before all the creatures God has generated
> from himself a rational potency that the

33 Cfr. a tal proposito P.A. CASAMASSA, *Gli apologisti greci, studio introduttivo*, Roma 1944; S. LILLA, *Introduzione al medioplatonismo*, Roma 1992; G. GIRGENTI, *Giustino martire. Il primo cristiano platonico. Con in appendice "Atti del martirio di San Giustino"*, Milano 1995.

Spirit Holy now calls glory of the Lord, now son, now wisdom, now angel, now God. (...).[34]

Also in the 1*Apology* 13,3-4 Justin affirms the divinity of the Spirit Holy, who belongs to God and it places him to the third place:

(...) we have learned that he (Jesus Christus) is the son of the true God, and we honors him to the second place, and to the third place the prophetic Spirit. In this they believe to show our folly, saying that we give the second place, after the unchangeable and eternal God, creator of all the things.[35]

Athenagoras, from the presupposition that God is

---

34 GIUSTINO, *Dialogo con Trifone* 61,1. Ed. crit. M. MARCOVICH, *Iustini martyris. Dialogus cum Tryphone*, Berlin-New-York 1997, pp. 174-175. Trad. di G. VISONÀ, *Dialogo con Trifone*, p. 217.

35 Ed. crit. M. MARCOVICII, *Iustini martyris. Apologiae pro christianis*, p. 51. Trad. di A.R. RACCONE, *Giustino. Le due apologie*, p. 57. Cfr. anche per il pensiero dei Padri apologisti e degli altri Padri J. LEBRETON, *Histoire du dogme de la Trinité*, voll. I-II, Paris 1927-28; Y. CONGAR, *Credo nello Spirito Santo*, vol. I. *Rivelazione e esperienze dello Spirito*, vol. III. *Teologia dello Spirito Santo*, Brescia 1984.1987.

non created and eternal, it deduces of it that also the Spirit Holy is an entity divine alien from all what is material and it's also distinguished by God Father, because from him it comes (ἀπορρεύει):

> On this reasoning it agrees also the prophetic Spirit: "The Lord, it says, it created me beginning of his streets for his works" (Pv 8,22). In truth also the same Spirit Holy who inspired those who proclaimed prophecies we say that it is emanation (ἀπόρροια) of God, who radiates himself and it reappears as ray of sun. 5. Who would not stay perplexed after have felt that are defined atheists those who recognize God Father and God Son and the Spirit Holy and who show of it the potency in the unity and the distinction in the order?.[36]

Athenagoras clarifies, in comparison with Justin, the role of the Spirit Holy in the eternity before the

36 ATENAGORA, *Supplica per i cristiani* 10,4-5. Ed. crit. M. MARCOVICH, *Athenagoras. Legatio pro christianis*, Berlin-New-York 1990, p. 41. Trad. di C. BURINI, *Gli apologeti greci*, Roma 1986, p. 262.

creation of the world. The Spirit Holy, Athenagoras tells tuning with Justin, it's the one who unites the Father with the Son and, as such, it comes to be the third in order of degree:

> and since the Son is in the Father and the Father in the Son in the unity and in the potency of the Spirit; mind and verb of the Father is God's son. 5. Who would not stay perplexed after having felt that atheists are defined those who recognize God Father and God Son and the Spirit Holy and who show of it the potency in the unity and the distinction in the order?.[37]

To such regard it is pertinent the consideration of C. MORESCHINI:

> it's Athenagoras who, only among all the apologists, it's put the problem of the origin of the Spirit Holy by the Father: if he says that the Spirit is ἀπόρροια, evidently it not

---

37 ATENAGORA, *Supplica per i cristiani* 10,2.5. Ed. crit. M. MARCOVICH, *Athenagoras. Legatio pro christianis*, pp. 39-41. Trad. di C. BURINI, *Gli apologeti greci*, pp. 261-262.

only distinguishes him by the Son (…) but it also tries to understand how it can proceed by the Father without being the Son.[38]

Also Teophilus of Antioch, faithful to the triadic scheme of his predecessors, it brings out that the wisdom, identified with the Spirit Holy, is preexisting because coeternal to God, and, together with God Father and with the Son, forms the trinity:

Since God had his own immanent verb in his own heart, he him generated together with his wisdom emanating him before all the other things (…). This therefore, being God's spirit, principle, wisdom and potency of God, went down on the prophets and through them it spoke of the creation of the world and of all the other things. The prophets didn't exist when the world was created, but existed the wisdom of God that is in him and his holy verb who always

38 C. MORESCHINI, *Tradizione e innovazione nella pneumatologia di Tertulliano*, in "Augustinianum" 20 (1980), p. 642.

exists with him.[39]

It is to notice that the apologists employ the term spirit to indicate the third person of the trinity; term that in hellenistic field, above all stoic, it came to indicate the igneous spirit, of material nature, that unites and that vivifies all the things: the spirit is constitutive principle of the world, understood as force organic of material nature that necessarily puts in order the matter, it penetrates it, organizing the world.[40]

On the basis of the fact that the Spirit Holy is coeternal to God, because precedent the creation of the world, Tatian, countering the stoic position, affirms that the divine nature of the Spirit, as that one of the Father, is of transcendent order, not of material order, because God is Spirit:

> doesn't spread through the matter, but it is
> the one who gives order to the spirits of the

39 TEOFILO DI ANTIOCHIA, *ad Autolico* II,10. Ed. crit. M. MARCOVICH, *Tatiani Oratio. Ad Graecos. Theophili Antiocheni. Ad Autolycum*, Berlin-New-York 1995, pp. 53. Trad. di C. BURINI, *Gli apologeti greci*, p. 391.

40 M.I. PARENTE (a cura di), *Stoici antichi*, vol. I, Torino 1989, p. 131. Per l'influsso dello stoicismo nei Padri Apologisti vedi anche M. SPANNEUT, *Le stoicisme des Pères de l'église de Clément de Rome a Clement d'Alexandrie*, Paris 1957.

matter and to the forms that are in it, invisible and ineffable, also being he himself Father of the sensible and visible things.[41]

Tatian therefore confirms the transcendence atemporal of the divine spirit towards the matter, since God creates the forms in the matter but doesn't produce them from the matter, as instead the stoic ones sustain, why God is the constitutive element.[42] On the model of the stoic concept of Spirit, who is the principle from which all the things have origin, Athenagoras specifies that the Spirit Holy is the one who holds the creation, since "*every thing has been created and it is holded from its spirit*".[43]

41 TAZIANO, *La supplica ai Greci* 4,3. Ed. crit. M. MARCOVICH, *Tatiani Oratio. Ad Graecos. Theophili Antiocheni. Ad Autolycum*, p. 12. Trad. di C. BURINI, *Gli apologeti greci*, p. 188.
42 TAZIANO, *La supplica ai Greci* 4,1-2. Ed. crit. M. MARCOVICH, *Tatiani, Oratio ad Graecos. Theophili Antiocheni, Ad Autolycum*, p. 12.
43 ATENAGORA, *Supplica per i cristiani* 6,2. Ed. crit. M. MARCOVICH, *Athenagoras. Legatio pro christianis*, pp. 32. Trad. di C. BURINI, *Gli apologeti greci*, p. 257.

2.3. *The identity of the prophetic Spirit and of the reality prophetic*

In his *apology* 1,38,1-5 Justin affirms that the Spirit, who has spoken through the prophet Isaiah and of the author of the Psalms, it is the Verb of God. Also Plato, according to Justin

> has taken out from ours teacher – we intend to say from the words of the prophets – the affirmation according to which God, treating the amorphous matter, made the world, listened the precise words of Moses, whom we have already shown to be the first prophet and more ancient than the greek writers: 2. through him the prophetic spirit, revealing in which manner, to the origin, and from which elements God has created the world, he said in this way: "At the origin God created the sky and the earth. The earth was invisible and shapeless, and darkness on the abyss; and the Spirit of God went on the waters. And God said – be the light – and so

it was" (Gen 1,1-3).[44]

Justin, from the fact that the one who have spoken for mouth of Moses has been the Son of God, who is also denominated messenger and envoyed from the Father and not the Father, as instead the jews thought, it affirms that the jews have been reproached by the prophetic spirit, who is the same Christ, to not have recognized neither the Father nor the Son.[45]

Justin in *1apology* 59,1-4, it refers to Plato, who, for Justin, has been inspired by the verb who, as we have previously seen, it is wisdom of the Father, it believes that before the arrival of the verb in the flesh Plato was participating of the Logos.

In *1apology* 46,2-3 Justin affirms that the ancient greek wise men, considered atheists, were instead christians because they lived according to the reason, reflex and image of the divine reason that it is the wisdom of the Father:

it has been taught to us that Christ is the first-

44 GIUSTINO, *Apologia* I,59,1-2. Ed. crit. M. MARCOVICH, *Iustini martyris. Apologiae pro christianis*, p. 51. Trad. di A.R. RACCONE, *Giustino. Le due apologie*, pp. 114-115.
45 GIUSTINO, *Apologia* I,63,1-2. Ed. crit. M. MARCOVICH, *Iustini martyris. Apologiae pro christianis*, p. 121.

born of God, and we have already shown that he is the Logos whose it was participating the whole human species. And those who lived according to the Logos are christian, even if atheists were judged, as, among the greek, Socrates and Heraclitus and others as them.[46]

In the *2Apology* 8,1-2.10,2-6 Justin explains that as much as of truth and of well the ancient philosophers have enunciated it's the product of their rational activity, fruit for Justin of the presence of a part of the Logos:

> we know that have been hated and killed also the followers of the doctrine stoic, as, for some way, also the poet – at least when they are appeared moderate in the theme of the ethics, because of the semen of the Logos that is innate in every human birth: for instance, Heraclitus, as we have said, and, to our times, Musonius and others. As in fact we have shown, the demons have always operated so that it were hated those who, anyway, strive

46 Ed. crit. M. MARCOVICH, *Iustini martyris. Apologiae pro christianis*, p. 97. Trad. di A.R. RACCONE, *Giustino. Le due apologie*, p. 98.

to live according to the Logos, and to run away the evil". 10,2-6: "in fact all what straightly they enunciated and they found philosophers and legislators, in them it is fruit of search and speculation, because of a part of Logos. But since didn't know the Logos in his entirety, who is Christ, they are often contradicted also. Those who lived before Christ and strove to investigate and to investigate the things with the reason, according to the human possibilities, they were dragged in front of the courts as cruel and too much curious. One who more than every other tended to this, Socrates, was accused some same guilts that are imputed to us: in fact they said that he introduced new divinities, and that didn't believe in the gods that the city believed as such. He taught to the men instead to refuse the wicked demons, authors of the impieties narrated by the poets, doing to send away from the republic both Homer and the other poets, it also tried to push them to the knowledge of the God to them unknown, through the rational search. It said: «It is not easy to find the Father and creator of the universe, neither it is sure that the one who has found him it reveal him to all the men». This is what made our Christ with his potency. In fact to Socrates nobody believed until the point to die for this doctrine.[47]

For Justin therefore it is the Logos who gives the "*seeds*" of the reason to the ancient philosophers because, having been generated by the mind of the Father, it is he himself full of the wisdom of the Father. Insofar the Logos emits these "*seeds*" partial of his rich rationality through the action of the Spirit who, since wisdom of the Father, reveals the rational potency of the Logos to the men of good will, favoring their reception. The action of the Logos therefore for Justin is not separated by that one any Spirit, on the contrary it is intimately connected to it. The Logos reveals his rational

47 Ed. crit. M. MARCOVICH, *Iustini martyris. Apologiae pro christianis*, pp. 149.151-152. Trad. di A.R. RACCONE, *Giustino. Le due apologie*, pp. 144.146-147.

potency in the Spirit who illuminates every man, giving to every one a small spark of those ones are the teachings of the Father, contained in his divine mind and that the Logos has the assignment to mediate through the action of the Spirit who illuminates. This concept will be taken again by Clement of Alexandria, for whom the wisdom of the ancient ones is propedeutical to the true philosophy, that is fulfilled and definitely realized with the coming of the Verb in the flesh:

> So, before the coming of the Lord the philosophy was to the Greek necessary to reach the justice; it now becomes useful to reach the religion: it is in certain way a propedeutical for those who intend to conquer themselves the faith because of rational demonstration (...). 29,1: "One is, yes, the road of the truth, but in it, as in a perennial river, so many rivulets flow, one by one side one by the other. And then here are the divine words: "Listen, my son, and welcome my discourse, because you have a lot of streets of life: I teach you streets of

wisdom, because doesn't come you less the sources", which spring from the same earth. And certain not for a correct man only has enumerated more streets of salvation, on the contrary it adds that a lot of other streets there are for many correct, proclaiming: "The streets of the correct ones shine as light". Well, also the precepts and the propedeutiches can be streets and addresses of life.[48]

Always for Clement of Alexandria the Logos acts as pedagogue through the law of Moses and the prophets: in fact the Logos given to the man the law of Moses, to conduct him to the definitive salvation that is Christ.[49] Origen will explain better still this relationship of dependence of the man from the Logos, because of the reason. To such regard Origen specifies that the human

48 CLEMENTE ALESSANDRINO, *Stromati* I,5,28,1-29,1-3. Ed. crit. O. STÄHLIN, *Clemens Alexandrinus. Stromata*, Berlin 1960, pp. 17-18. Trad. di G. PINI, *Clemente Alessandrino. Stromati. Note di vera filosofia*, Milano 1985, pp. 90-91.
49 CLEMENTE ALESSANDRINO, *Pedagogo* I,7,60,1-3. Ed. crit. H.I. MARROU-M. HARL, *Clément d'Alexandrie. Le Pédagogue*, Paris 1960, pp. 216-218.

beings are provided with reason because the son, since wisdom of the Father, has transmitted it to the rational beings in proportional manner to their degree of holiness:

> The son God's generated only, through whom (…) have been done all the visible and invisible things (…) has made participate invisibly of himself all the rational creatures, so that each participated of him as much as it adhered to him with love.[50]

Returning to Justin he believes that what has been revealed it is already reality, as in the case of the prophecy of Is 53,1.7 on the passion of Jesus, since the prophetic spirit is the Verb of God.[51]

For Justin therefore the prophetic Spirit, that is the Verb, is tense to announce the most important events of the life of Jesus and the most meaningful facts.[52]

---

50 ORIGENE, *Principii* II,6,3. Ed. crit. H. CROUZEL-M. SIMONETTI, *Origène. Traité des principes*, Paris 1978, p. 314. Trad. di M. SIMONETTI, *I Principi di Origene*, Torino 1968, p. 286.

51 GIUSTINO, *Dialogo con Trifone* 114,2. Ed. crit. M. MARCOVICH, *Iustini martyris. Dialogus cum Tryphone*, Berlin-New-York 1997, pp. 265-266. Vedi anche GIUSTINO, *1Apologia* 42,1-4. Ed. crit. M. MARCOVICH, *Iustini martyris. Apologiae pro christianis*, p. 91.

52 GIUSTINO, *1Apologia* 32,1-2.7-8;39,1-2;41,1-4. Ed. crit.

2.4. *The function of the Spirit in the incarnation of Jesus: the first coming of the Spirit*

Justin, connecting himself to the prophecy of Isaia 11,1-2 affirms that this passage is applied to Christ, to whom the potencies of the Spirit are been given, as are enumerated in Is 11,1-3. Justin counters Tryphon affirming

> that the virtues of the Spirit here enumerated have not gone down on him as if it needed of it, but as to find rest in him, that is to say to establish with him a limit so that didn't rise no prophets in breast to your race, as it happened for the past, and this we can ascertain it with your eyes, because after him between you not has risen more even a prophet (…). The Spirit therefore has rested, that is to say he is stopped with the coming of the one after whose, once realized his economy among the men, it had to stop among you, and to find instead of new in him rest.[53]

M. MARCOVICH, *Iustini martyris. Apologiae pro christianis*, pp. 78-79.87.90.
53 GIUSTINO, *Dialogo con Trifone* 87,2-3.5. Ed. crit. M.

The first testimony of the fact that Jesus didn't need any gifts of the Spirit because with him it had to stop, it is for Justin the same birth of Jesus, birth where Jesus was already provided with a proper potency:

> Since the birth in fact it was provided with the potency that is him proper, then, growing, as all the other men and using of time in time the convenient things, it assigned to the various tappes of the growth what it was proper to every one (...).[54]

With regard to this event Justin takes again the text of Lc 1,35 and he affirms that the Spirit Holy is the one who has approached himself to Mary, because with his potency she was pregnant.[55]

Here Justin identifies the Spirit and the virtue of God with the Logos. It was this Spirit (Logos) who made pregnant

MARCOVICH, *Iustini martyris. Dialogus cum Tryphone*, pp. 221-222. Trad. di G. VISONÀ, *Dialogo con Trifone*, pp. 276-277. Vedi anche *Dialogo con Trifone* 88,1. Ed. crit. M. MARCOVICH, *Iustini martyris. Dialogus cum Tryphone*, p. 222.

54 GIUSTINO, *Dialogo con Trifone* 88,2. Ed. crit. M. MARCOVICH, *Iustini martyris. Dialogus cum Tryphone*, pp. 222-223. Trad. di G. VISONÀ, *Dialogo con Trifone*, p. 278.

55 GIUSTINO, *1Apologia* 33,4-5. Ed. crit. M. MARCOVICH, *Iustini martyris. Apologiae pro christianis*, p. 80.

Mary not for contest of man, but for the virtue of God.

2.5. *The function of the Spirit in the church*

2.5.1. The second coming of the Spirit

Finished the terrestrial life of Jesus, for Justin the virtues of the Spirit stop "to rest" in Him, because these same virtues are reconverted in gifts, that Christ will give to every one some believers because of the potency of the Spirit:

> (...) the gifts that had been prophesied and that for the grace of the potency of that Spirit he grants to those who believe in him, according to what he knows that every one is worthy of it. I have already said, and I repeat it, that had been prophesied that this would have happened as for his after the ascension to the sky. Has said therefore the Writing: "He is ascended upwards doing prisoners, he has distributed gifts to the men". And in a another prophecy it is said: "And it will happen that after these things I will emit my Spirit on every flesh, on my servants and on my

servants, and they will prophesy". From us it is possible see both women and men who have received charismas by the Spirit of God.[56]

Justin, quoting the prophecy of Sal 68,19 and Gl 3,1-2, it is placed in line of continuity with the *Epistle to the Ephesians* 4,8 where Sal 68,19 is cited for testifying that Jesus, ascending to the sky, has distributed the charismas on the believers according to the measure of the gift of Christ. For this writing is:

> Ascending in the sky has brought with himself the prisoners, he has distributed gifts to the men" (Sal 68,19) (…). It is him that established some as apostles, others as prophets etc (Ef 4,7-13).

It is important to notice, to such intention, that the donation of the charismas both in the *Epistle to the Ephesians* and in the *dialogue with Trypho* one realize in the one who is already believer. Then this donation is realized in the one who is become member of the church

---

56 GIUSTINO, *Dialogo con Trifone* 87,5-6-88,1. Ed. crit. M. MARCOVICH, *Iustini martyris. Dialogus cum Tryphone*, p. 222. Trad. di G. VISONÀ, *Dialogo con Trifone*, pp. 277-278.

through his profession of faith, that is carried out in the baptism as it underlines E. NORELLI, commenting the *Epistle to Diognetus* in 11,5:

> The believers who obtain the knowledge of the mysteries are the disciples, that are not identified certain with "who must choose still to approach and to listen" - it seems to be about of a more elevated teaching, presumably established upon the exegesis of the Writing, that is imparted to any believers already baptized and deriving probably from the paganism.[57]

2.5.2. The function baptismal-eucharistical of the Spirit

As a result of the fact that the blood of Jesus doesn't derive from human semen but from the divine potency for work of the Spirit Holy, Justin affirms that this blood is source of salvation for the believers. It is source of salvation because in the blood of Christ it is present the potency of the Spirit Holy, because whose Jesus gives the

57 E. NORELLI (a cura di), *A Diogneto*, Milano 1991, pp. 127-128 n. 17.

remission of the sins; remission that the Spirit Hoy had
prophesied in Gen 49,11:

> As for the prophecy patriarch's Jacob
> registered by Moses – "washes in the wine
> his dress, in the blood of the grape his
> mantle" (Gen 49,11) -, it indicated that he
> would have washed in his blood the believers
> in him. The Spirit Holy, in fact, with "dress",
> has designated those who would have
> obtained for his means the remission of the
> sins; in them he is continually present with
> his potency, and it will openly be him in his
> second coming. Saying then "the grape's
> blood", the word has shown, through the
> artifice of the image, that Christ has some
> blood, not however from human semen, on
> the contrary from the potency of God.[58]

Then the Spirit Holy assumes here the role of
coordinator because, through the blood of Christ, be given

---

58 GIUSTINO, *Dialogo con Trifone* 54,1-2. Ed. crit. M.
MARCOVICH, *Iustini martyris. Dialogus cum Tryphone*, pp.
158-159. Trad. di G. VISONÀ, *Dialogo con Trifone*, pp. 199-
200.

to the believers the remission of the sins. With regard to always the baptism, Justin denominates this washing "illumination", since the spirit of the baptized one is illuminated by the Spirit Holy in the mind:

> This washing is called illumination, since those who understand these things are illuminated in the mind. And the one who must have illuminated it is washed in the name of Jesus Christus, crucified under Pontius Pilate, and in the name of the Spirit Holy, who has preannounced through the prophets all the events concerning Jesus.[59]

Also here the Spirit Holy is the principal agent of the illumination of the mind. Through this washing the baptized one, free from the sins, welcomes the light of the Spirit Holy. In Justin it is in embryonic sense the concept of illumination that will be developed by Clement of Alexandria, who will say that

> in this way we, baptized once, sweep away

---

59 GIUSTINO, *Apologia* I,61,8. Ed. crit. Ed. crit. M. MARCOVICH, *Iustini martyris. Apologiae pro christianis*, p. 119. Trad. di A.R. RACCONE, *San Giustino. Le due apologie,* p. 111.

the sins that, to form of cloud, made shade to the divine Spirit and we make in such way free, without impediments and luminous the eye of the Spirit, who only allows to us to contemplate the divinity, because of the Spirit Holy who up some sky flows in us.[60]

In the liturgical practice of the first christian communities, tightly connected to the baptism, it is the liturgy eucharistical. In fact Justin refers to the Spirit Holy not only regarding the prayer eucharistical but also the invocation (epiclesi), where God Father is invoked because he sends the Spirit Holy both on the elements of the bread and of the wine, because be consecrated, and on the believers to sanctify them through the communion.[61]

To the Spirit Holy also it's up for Justin the function of consecration during the invocation (epiclesi), so that the elements of the bread and of the wine be transformed into

60 CLEMENTE ALESSANDRINO, *Pedagogo* I,28,1. Ed. crit. H.I. MARROU - M. HARL, *Clément d'Alexandrie. Le Pédagogue*, p. 162. Trad. di D. TESSORE, *Clemente Alessandrino. Il Pedagogo*, Roma 2005, p. 61.

61 GIUSTINO, *1Apologia* 65,1-3.5. Ed. crit. M. MARCOVICH, *Iustini martyris. Apologiae pro christianis*, pp. 125-126. Vedi anche a tal proposito S. FELICI (a cura di), *Spirito Santo e catechesi patristica*, Roma 1983, pp. 195-208.

body and blood of Christ.

2.5.3. The gifts of the Spirit

Tightly associated to the practice of the baptism it is the effusion of the gifts that, as we have seen, it happens after Christ ascended to the sky (Dial 87-88). justin underlines in *Dialogue* 39,2-4, referring to Is 11,1-2, that to those who have been baptized, Christ will impart the gifts of the Spirit according to their dignity. Also in the *Epistle to Diognetus* 11,5 the gift of the grace is emitted on the saints to be precise in those who already believe in the trinity and in the church. The Spirit of intelligence, quoted in *Dialogue* 39,2 it also recurs in the *Epistle to Diognetus* 11,5 and in 12,9. In 11,5 the intelligence conferred by the grace, that alludes to the Spirit Holy for some researchers, while for others in line with E. NORELLI, alludes "to the grace of the church that accompanies the come loosing some plan of salvation continuing the work of the grace of the prophets",[62] it is intended, according to E. NORELLI, as *"the ability to understand the divine mysteries also through an*

---

62 E. NORELLI (a cura di), *A Diogneto*, p. 127 n.17.

understanding christological of the Writings".[63]

In the *Epistle to Diogneto* 12,9 is affirmed that "*the apostles are provided with intelligence*".[64]

This signifies, according to E. NORELLI, that "*the apostles are therefore able to understand, without doubt the hidden sense, christological of the Writings*".[65]

2.5.4. The function of the Spirit in the ascent of the soul to God: the diakonia of the Spirit

The gifts of the Spirit have been emitted on the church so that every faithful with his charisma competes to form, together with the others, an united church in the Spirit having Christ as head. Therefore the Spirit comes to be the guarantor of the union between every believer and Christ, his head. In such perspective one place the reflection of Tatian of the Spirit deacon. Tatian, from the

---

63 E. NORELLI (a cura di), *A Diogneto*, p. 128 n.18.
64 Ed. crit. F. XAVER FUNK-K. BIHLMEYER-M. WHITTAKER, *Die Apostolischen Väter. Griechisch-deutsche Parallelausgabe,* p. 322. Trad. di E. NORELLI, *A Diogneto*, p. 131.
65 E. NORELLI (a cura di), *A Diogneto*, p. 134 n.19. Cfr. anche MELITONE, *Sulla Pasqua* 40-45. Ed. crit. O. Perler, *Méliton de Sardes. Sur la Pâque et fragments*, Paris 1966, pp. 80-84.

stoic thought, according to which only the Spirit is contained in all the beings of the creation and therefore also in the man, affirms that the soul in itself is deadly, tense to the death, however if it is in couple with the Spirit doesn't die because through the Spirit it can ascend upwards, in the celestial regions.[66]

The espression "*servant of the God that has suffered (* διάκονον τοῦ πεποιηκότος θεοῦ)", reported to the Spirit, it is to indicate for Tatian that through the Spirit Holy, who is the "servant", the soul reaches the immortality and the eternal incorruptibility. The expression "*spirit servant*" (πνεῦμα διάκονος) had been employed by the gnostics basilidians-valentinians, to indicate that the Spirit has the function of deacon, because it communicates to Jesus, as in the case of the baptism, the strength that he receives from the pneumatic Christ.[67]

Clement of Alexandria will explain better the role of the Spirit deacon who has one own identity christological

66 TAZIANO, *Discorso ai Greci* 13. Ed. crit. M. MARCOVICH, *Tatiani Oratio. Ad Graecos. Theophili Antiocheni. Ad Autolycum*, p. 30.
67 Vedi a tal proposito F. BOLGIANI, Διακονία τοῦ πνεῦματος - *Fortuna e sfortuna di una formula teologica,* in "Augustinianum" 20 (1980), p. 531.

and anthropological, since it comes to be not only the support, the strength of the Logos, but also the support of the soul because this reaches the incorruptibility and the immortality.[68]

Therefore both Tatian and Clement of Alexandria, inheriting the gnostic conception of the Spirit deacon, give to the Spirit a subordinate connotation in comparison to the Father and to the son, as besides one notice in Justin. In fact also Justin, together with the other apologists, it places the Spirit to the third place in order of dignity.

---

68 CLEMENTE ALESSANDRINO, *Pedagogo* II,2,19,3-20,1. Ed. crit. C. MONDÉSERT-H.I. MARROU, *Clément d'Alexandrie. Le Pédagogue*, Paris 1965, pp. 46-48. Per il pensiero di Clemente alessandrino sullo Spirito vedi V. MESSANA, *Lo Spirito Santo e l'accezione clementina di senso spirituale*, in "Augustinianum" 20 (1980), pp. 485-497.

3. THE HEURISTIC ASPECTS OF THE FUNCTION AND OF THE IDENTITY OF THE PNEUMA IN IRENAEUS OF LYONS

3.1. *The divine connotation of the Spirit in the eternal plan of God*

3.1.1. The divine nature of the Spirit Holy

In front of the spread of the first three heresies, the gnosticism, the marcionism and the montanism, Irenaeus of Lions, native of Asia Minor, toward the end of the II century d.C., came down in field to disprove these heresies, writing a work of vast breath entitled "*Against heresies*", and a modest catechism for the adults entitled "*Epideixis*" (*Demonstration of the apostolic preaching*). Irenaeus of Lyons, come to knowledge of the spread some gnostic heresy valentinian, according to which under to the sovereign God it existed a series of divine beings of decreasing order, among whom also the Spirit Holy,[69] referring to the prophecy of Is 57,16, it affirms the divinity of the Spirit who, since eternal, it is in the Father before the creation of the

_____

69 Cfr. A. ORBE, *La teologia dei secoli II-III, il confronto della grande chiesa con lo gnosticismo*, Roma 1995, pp. 109-112.

world.[70]

For Irenaeus therefore the Spirit is of the same rank of the Father and, distinguished by the Father, occupies the third place, without this implicates his subordination, as the same Irenaeus declares in *Demonstration of the Apostolic Preaching* 6. From this text emerge also the essential activities that characterize the Spirit: he prophesies, it knows God and it conducts the correct ones for the street of the justice. Irenaeus, in the "*Against heresies*" IV,20,3, identifies, on the track of Teophilus of Antioch, the Spirit Holy also with the wisdom. Identifying the wisdom with the Spirit, Irenaeus, as affirms A. Gervais "*it notices better still this eternal presence of the Holy Spirit near God*".[71]

3.1.2. The Spirit anoints the Logos

Another characteristic, pertaining to the divinity of the Spirit, is for Irenaeus the unction of the Verb. Irenaeus affirms that the Spirit Holy, since eternal, it is

70 IRENEO, *Controleeresie* V,12,3. Ed.crit. A.ROUSSEAU - L. DOUTRELEAU -CH. MERCIER, *Irénée de Lyon*, Paris 1969, pp. 144-146.
71 A. GERVAIS, *Les missions divines de St. Justin à Origène*, Fribourg 1958, p. 65.

the oil with which the Father consecrates the Son.[72]

The Father for Irenaeus anoints the Son through the oil of the unction, that is the Spirit from the eternity. Irenaeus is placed on the same line of Justin and Barnabas, who had foreseed a some identification of the Spirit with the unction, from the reading of Is 6,11. For Irenaeus therefore the Spirit becomes the consecration, the Son is the consecrate one and the Father consecrates the Son through the Spirit who is the oil of the unction.[73]

In *Demonstration of the Apostolic Preaching* 53 Irenaeus affirms that the Son of God has received the appellative of Christ or Anointed, besides that one of Jesus who signifies savior since it has been anointed from the spirit of God, in sight of his incarnation and of his message of salvation that had to announce to the men.

---

72 IRENEO, *Dimostrazione della predicazione apostolica* 47. Ed. crit. A. ROUSSEAU, *Irénée de Lyon. Démonstration de la prédication apostolique*, Paris 1995, p. 152.
73 IRENEO, *Contro le eresie* III,18,3. Ed. crit. A. ROUSSEAU-L. DOUTRELEAU, *Irénée de Lyon. Contre les hérésies*, Paris 2002, pp. 350-352.

3.2. *The function of the Spirit in the creation of the world*

3.2.1. The Spirit Holy modeler of the material universe

Irenaeus affirms that God creates the material world through his Verb who is the archetype, while the Spirit, identified with the term wisdom, it has the function to order it, so that the various parts that compose the world are in harmony between them and are developed according to their intrinsic qualities, emitting all their own potentialities.[74]

3.2.2. The Spirit Holy coordinator of the spiritual potencies

Concerning the creation of the spiritual potencies that populate the seven skies, the Spirit Holy has for Irenaeus the assignment to distribute his seven gifts according to these seven skies, adapting these charismas according to the order of the skies and making

---

74 IRENEO, *Dimostrazione della predicazione apostolica* 5. Ed. crit. A. ROUSSEAU, *Irénée de Lyon. Démonstration de la prédication apostolique*, p. 90.

them correspond in decreasing way.[75]

3.2.3. The Spirit Holy the man's finisher

As regards the creation of the man, Irenaeus affirms that the man is created to resemblance of God by the hands of the Father, through the Son and the Spirit.[76] Irenaeus explains that the Spirit Holy has the function to form the perfect man, so that resemble to God. The perfect man is for Irenaeus the man who participates some Spirit of the Father, to whom has been given a body moulded to image of God.[77] The Spirit Holy therefore has the assignment for Irenaeus to make the man alike to the Father, to transform him because can be similar to the Father. The Spirit Holy also has the function to resuscitate the body of the believers to introduce it in the kingdom of God. [78]

---

75 IRENEO, *Dimostrazione della predicazione apostolica* 9. Ed. crit. A. ROUSSEAU, *Irénée de Lyon. Démonstration de la prédication apostolique*, p. 96.
76 IRENEO, *Contro le eresie* V,6,1. Ed. crit. A. ROUSSEAU-L. DOUTRELEAU-CH. MERCIER, *Irénée de Lyon. Contre les hérésies,* p. 72.
77 IRENEO, *Contro le eresie* V,6,1. Ed. crit. A. ROUSSEAU-L. DOUTRELEAU-CH. MERCIER, *Irénée de Lyon. Contre les hérésies,* pp. 74-76.
78 IRENEO, *Dimostrazione della predicazione apostolica* 42.

3.3. *The function and the prefigurations of the Spirit Holy in the history of the old Testament*

3.3.1. The prefigurations of the Spirit in the old Testament

Irenaeus uses the image of the dew, diffused on all the earth, to preannounce the gift of the Spirit Holy on Jesus, who in turn has given this gift to the church, sending from the sky the Spirit:

> (…) while on all the earth there would have been the dew, that is to say the Spirit of God, who is come down on the Lord: "Spirit of wisdom and intelligence, Spirit of suggestion and fortitude, Spirit of science and pity, Spirit of fear of God (Is 11,2-3). In turn the Lord has given him to the church, sending from the skies the Spirit (…) on all the earth, where, as the Lord says, the devil has been thrown as the lightning (…).[79]

Ed. crit. A. ROUSSEAU, *Irénée de Lyon. Démonstration de la prédication apostolique,* pp. 140-142.
79 IRENEO, *Contro le eresie* III,17,3. Ed. crit. A. ROUSSEAU-L. DOUTRELEAU, *Irénée de Lyon. Contre les hérésies,* pp. 334-336. Trad. di GERARDO DI NOLA, *Lo Spirito Santo*, p. 190.

3.3.2. The prophetic prediction of the Spirit

According to Irenaeus the old Testament is come as the new Testament for work of the Spirit Holy, who talks through the prophets and it guides the history of the old Testament toward his accomplishment with the coming of the Verb.[80] In fact the Spirit Holy for Irenaeus preannounces, during the history old-testamentary, as would have been the coming of the Lord. In the *Against heresies* III,21,4 Irenaeus affirms that the Spirit Holy has preannounced, through the prophets, the birth of Jesus, the fullness of the times and the coming of the kingdom of God, Irenaeus also affirms in *Demonstration of the Apostolic Preaching* 86 that the prophets Isaiah and David preannounced the future missionary activity of the disciples. Then in the chapters 87-95 are presented other prophetic preannouncements of the Spirit, as the supremacy of the love (*Demonstration of the Apostolic Preaching* 87), the salvation in the name of Christ (*Demonstration of the Apostolic Preaching* 88), the supremacy of the Spirit and the new life in the Spirit

---

80 IRENEO, *Dimostrazione della predicazione apostolica* 5. Ed. crit. A. ROUSSEAU, *Irénée de Lyon. Démonstration de la prédication apostolique,* p. 90.

(*Demonstration of the Apostolic Preaching* 89-90), the pagan's place in the church (*Demonstration of the Apostolic Preaching* 91.92), the church, the synagogue and the welcome of the pagans in the church (*Demonstration of the Apostolic Preaching* 94-95).

3.4. *The role of the Spirit in the incarnation of the Verb*

3.4.1. The Spirit divine potency who gives life during the incarnation

Especially in *Demonstration of the Apostolic Preaching* 40 Irenaeus confers to the Spirit a determining role in the conception of the Verb:

> The one therefore who is announced by Moses and by the prophets of the highest and almighty God, Father of the universe, source of every thing, who conversed with Moses, it came in the Judea, generated by God because of the Spirit Holy, and been born by the virgin Mary of the family of David and of Abraham, Jesus, the anointed one of God, who has revealed himself as the one who had already been predicted from

the prophets.[81]

Irenaeus shows therefore the Spirit as the one who not only has anointed Jesus before the creation of the world, but who has also preannounced, for mouth of the prophets, the coming of the Verb and, as such, he is the same one who has realized the incarnation of the Verb in the breast of Mary. The Spirit therefore for Irenaeus it is the one who unites the event of the incarnation of the Verb to that one of his eternal generation:

> There were sent by God, through the Spirit Holy, the prophets, who admonished the people and they brought again him to the almighty God of the Fathers, made heralds of the revelation of our Lord Jesus Christus, Son of God, announcing that from the progeny of Davide it would be flourished his body, so that be, according to the flesh Son of David – who was Son of Abraham – because of a long chain of generations, and

---

81 IRENEO, *Dimostrazione della predicazione apostolica* 40. Ed. crit. A. ROUSSEAU, *Irénée de Lyon. Démonstration de la prédication apostolique,* p. 138. Trad. di E. PERETTO, *Epideixis. Antico catechismo degli adulti*, Roma 1981, pp. 127-128.

according to the Spirit, God's Son, preexisting with the Father, generated before the construction of the world, and appeared to the whole world at the end of this epoch as man, him God's Verb, who "it recapitulates in himself all the things, those ones of the sky and those ones of the earth" (Ef 1,10).[82]

To the light of this Irenaeus adds that the Spirit Holy has brought the whole economy of salvation of the man to accomplishment through the incarnation of the Verb, who man is made himself, so that the human nature not be tense to the destruction but to the salvation:

the Spirit Holy, is come down therefore because of the pre-established economy of the salvation, while the son unique of God, who is also the Verb of the Father, come the fullness of the times, it is become incarnate in the man and because of the man. Jesus Christus our Lord who, as the Lord himself

82 IRENEO, *Dimostrazione della predicazione apostolica* 30. Ed. crit. A. ROUSSEAU, *Irénée de Lyon. Démonstration de la prédication apostolique,* p. 126. Trad. di E. PERETTO, *Epideixis. Antico catechismo degli adulti,* pp. 112-113.

attests is a only and the same one, (this Jesus Christus) whom the apostles confess and the prophets proclaim, has in fact brought to accomplishment the whole economy of salvation of the man (…).[83]

The Spirit therefore for Irenaeus has also a function of salvation with regard to the humanity of Christ and of the man; as the Verb has welcomed the Spirit in the flesh, so the man when it welcomes the Spirit in the flesh it becomes spiritual and he can possess the kingdom of God:

it is in fact the Spirit who brings to perfection all what he has to his disposition. Insofar if one takes such availability of the Spirit for the weakness of his own flesh, is major strength that what is strong overcome what it is weak, and so it happens that the weakness of the flesh is absorbed from the strength of the Spirit; besides, because of the

---

83 IRENEO, *Contro le eresie* III,17,4. Ed. crit. A. ROUSSEAU-L. DOUTRELEAU, *Irénée de Lyon. Contre les hérésies,* pp. 336-338. Trad. di GERARDO DI NOLA, *Lo Spirito Santo*, pp. 190-191.

communion of the Spirit, a man of the species is not more carnal, but spiritual. The flesh, therefore, without the Spirit Holy is dead, doesn't have in itself the life and, so, it cannot possess the kingdom of God.[84]

Irenaeus, from the antithetical parallelism of Jesus new Adam, it arrives to affirm that, with the incarnation, Jesus has renewed the destined humanity, before with Adam, to the death and now, with Jesus, to a new life, that one of the Spirit.[85]

3.4.2. The Spirit Holy consecrates Jesus in the baptism

Another meaningful event, in which the Spirit has a determining role in the life of Jesus is for Irenaeus

---

84 IRENEO, *Contro le eresie* V,9,2-3. Ed. crit. A. ROUSSEAU-L. DOUTRELEAU-CH. MERCIER, *Irénée de Lyon. Contre les hérésies,* p. 110. Trad. di GERARDO DI NOLA, *Lo Spirito Santo,* pp. 200-220. Vedi anche IRENEO, *Contro le eresie* V,6,1. Ed. crit. A. ROUSSEAU-L. DOUTRELEAU-CH. MERCIER, *Irénée de Lyon. Contre les hérésies,* pp. 72-80.

85 IRENEO, *Contro le eresie* III,18,2. Ed. crit. A. ROUSSEAU-L. DOUTRELEAU, *Irénée de Lyon. Contre les hérésies,* pp. 344-346. Cfr. anche *Dimostrazione della predicazione apostolica* 31-32. Ed. crit. A. ROUSSEAU, *Irénée de Lyon. Démonstration de la prédication apostolique,* pp. 126-128.

the event of the baptism.[86]

The Spirit Holy is come down on Jesus in the form of dove, to consecrate him with the purpose to propagate among the men the kingdom of God. Then the Spirit covers not only in the event of the baptism of Jesus the role of the one who consecrates, since it consecrates Jesus, but also that one of cooperator, because together with Jesus he was in the middle of the men of that time and together they undertake to fulfil the will of God in the men, who opened their heart to the new law preached by Christ with the potency of the Spirit. Irenaeus detains himself on the event of the baptism also in the *Against haeresies* III,9,3 and it underlines that Jesus is denominated Christ, because he has been anointed to bring the good announcement to the humbles ones, and to realize his mission of salvation. In manner different from Justin, for whom the unction is intended in sense atemporal as cause of the generation of the Verb, with reference to whom the unction shows his dignity of Son of God; for Irenaeus the unction is intended in the sense

---

86 IRENEO, *Contro le eresie* III,17,1. Ed. crit. A. ROUSSEAU-L. DOUTRELEAU, *Irénée de Lyon. Contre les hérésies,* pp. 328-330.

of a divine and anthropological manifestation, because the Spirit really goes down on the person of Jesus, so that Jesus realizes in the history the assignment to evangelize and to save the lost humanity in the abyss of the death.

3.5. *The role of the Spirit in the time of the church*

3.5.1. Spirit evangelical and of faith

Another consequent event to that one of the baptism of Jesus, where the Spirit has a determining role, is for Irenaeus the event of the Pentecost.[87] Here the Spirit purchases the role of protagonist of the history, because it is the one who guides the humanity toward the vital understanding of the Word of God and toward the unity. With the event of the Pentecost it begins for Irenaeus the mission evangelical of the apostles in the church, under the guide of the Spirit Holy: the church professes and teaches the evangelical message transmitted by the apostles[88] and it preaches a single and

---

87 IRENEO, *Contro le eresie* III,17,2. Ed. crit. A. ROUSSEAU-L. DOUTRELEAU, *Irénée de Lyon. Contre les hérésies,* pp. 330-334

88 IRENEO, *Contro le eresie* I,10,1. Ed. crit. A. ROUSSEAU-L. DOUTRELEAU, *Irénée de Lyon. Contre les hérésies,* Paris 1979, pp. 154-158.

same street of salvation.[89]

3.5.2. Spirit of unity

Complementary to the work evangelical of the apostles is for Irenaeus the unifying function of the Spirit in the church[90] This unifying activity of the Spirit is revealed in the church through the division and the distribution of the charismas on the believers, in such way that the believer, who participates of these gifts emitted by the Spirit, be placed not only in communion of life with Christ, who is the head of the church through whom one reaches the communion with God, but also with the brothers.[91]

---

89 IRENEO, *Contro le eresie* V,20,1. Ed. crit. A. ROUSSEAU-L. DOUTRELEAU-CH. MERCIER, *Irénée de Lyon. Contre les hérésies,* pp. 252-256.

90 IRENEO, *Contro le eresie* III,24,1. Ed Crit. A. ROUSSEAU - L. DOUTRELEAU, *Irénée de Lyon. Contre les hérésies,* pp. 472-474.

91 IRENEO, *Contro le eresie* III,11,8. Ed.crit. A. ROUSSEAU - L. DOUTRELEAU, *Irénée de Lyon. Contre les hérésies,* pp. 160-170.

3.6. *The role of the Spirit Holy in the life of the christian*

3.6.1. The residence of the Spirit in the man

Irenaeus, referring to the 1Cor 3,16-17, where it is called temple the body where it lives the Spirit Holy, it adds that our bodies are also temple of Christ, only when they persevere in a behaviour of life free from the contaminations.[92] Since limbs of Christ these bodies for Irenaeus will have part to the resurrection for the potency of God. In the *Against heresies* V,9,1-3 Irenaeus underlines that the body moulded by God cannot reach with the single his strength the salvation, without the aid of the Spirit. Those who place in their hearts the Spirit of God are raised to the divine life.[93] The role of the Spirit Holy is for Irenaeus that one to not only sanctify those who conduct an entire life, lived according to the sign of the purity and of the holiness, but also those who open their hearts to the action sanctifier of the Spirit.

---

92 IRENEO, *Contro le eresie* V,6,2. Ed. crit. A. ROUSSEAU - L. DOUTRELEAU-CH. MERCIER, *Irénée de Lyon. Contre les hérésies,* pp. 80-84.

93 IRENEO, *Contro le eresie* V,9,3. Ed. crit. A. ROUSSEAU - L. DOUTRELEAU-CH. MERCIER, *Irénée de Lyon. Contre les hérésies,* pp. 112-116.

3.6.2. The Spirit Holy advocate

The Spirit Holy for Irenaeus is the one who is called to be the middleman between sky and earth, because through of him the souls of those who save themselves reach the Son and through the Son they reach the Father. The advocate has therefore for Irenaeus the mission to conduct the souls to God, who has for them prepared a worthy abode according to their specific dignity.[94]

---

94 IRENEO, *Contro le eresie* V,36,2. Ed. Crit. A. ROUSSEAU - L. DOUTRELEAU-CH. MERCIER, *Irénée de Lyon. Contre les hérésies,* pp. 456-460.

4. THE HEURISTIC ASPECTS OF THE FUNCTION AND OF THE IDENTITY OF THE PNEUMA IN CLEMENT OF ALEXANDRIA, ORIGEN, TERTULLIAN AND CYPRIAN

4.1. *Origin and nature of the Spirit Holy: the Spirit Holy proceeds from the Father*

Origen, native of Alexandria, it is the maximum exponent of the alexandrine tradition that had as centre of meeting and cultural exchanges this city. He has been one of the greatest theologians of the beginning of the III century: his speculation mainly deals with the life trinitary and therefore also with the reality of the Spirit. Origen affirms that the nature of the Spirit is divine: he to such intention doesn't use, in polemic with the gnosticism valentinian, the concept of emanation (προβολή) because this denies the eternity of the divine nature of the Spirit. For Origen therefore the Spirit, since emitted by the Father, it must not be understood as separate because from him it comes. Ever since God for Origen it is spirit, he deduces of it that the Spirit, who comes from the Father, it is of divine nature.[95] In *Principles* 1,2,13

---

95 ORIGENE, *Principi* II,2,1. Ed. crit. H. CROUZEL-M. SIMONETTI, *Origène. Traité des principes*, Paris 1978, p.

Origen, from the image of the goodness that resides in God Father, affirms that the Son, generated by God Father, and the Spirit Holy, proceeding from God Father, reproduce both the nature of that goodness. Origen uses the term *"to proceed"* reported to the Spirit Holy to explain that the Spirit Holy has his origin from the Father, that is to say it comes from the Father. Always staying in the field of the utterance or of the emission of the Spirit from the Father, as we have seen in Origen, it is opportune here to mention Tertullian to do a comparison of it. Tertullian in the *Against Praxeas* 8 use the greek term utterance (προβολή) to fight the false knowledge, from which the term derives. In fact Tertullian opposes himself to the utterances of the gnostic Valentinus, why between emanation (προβολή) and God Father, from whom these come, doesn't exist identity of substance, as instead it is it for Tertullian but separation. Estranging

---

246. Sulla figura di Origene vedi J. DANIÉLOU, *Origène. La table ronde,* Paris 1948; A. MONACI CASTAGNO, *Origene. Dizionario, la cultura, il pensiero, le opere*, Roma 2000; M. SIMONETTI (a cura di), *Origene esegeta e la sua tradizione*, Morcelliana, Brescia 2004. Per il concetto di Spirito vedi F. BOLGIANI, *Spirito Santo*, in A. DI BERARDINO (a cura di), *Dizionario patristico e di antichità cristiane*, vol. II, Casale Monferrato 1983, col. 3285-3298.

himself from the gnostic thought of the utterance, Tertullian underlines the trinity of the persons Father, Son and Spirit Holy, prepared in decreasing sense, without for this to sacrifice of it the monarchy or better the oneness of substance.[96] To make clear this relationship of unity and of individuality, reported to the third person of the trinity, Tertullian uses the image of the ray that comes from the sun (*Apologetic* 21,11): as the ray is emitted from the sun and as such it is not separated from the substance of the sun because from this it comes, equally the Spirit, who has been emitted from the Father, is not separated from the Father because from this it comes. In *Against Praxeas* 4 Tertullian underlines also that the Spirit Holy derives from the Father through the Son, saving so the oneness of the substance of the divine persons. But Tertullian, if from a side it wants to save the unity of the substance that is common to the three divine persons, from the other one he wants to safeguard the otherity of the divine persons, affirming that these ones

---

96 TERTULLIANO, *Contro Prassea* 8,2-7. Ed. crit. G. SCARPAT, *Q.S.F. Tertulliano. Contro Prassea*, Torino 1985, pp. 158-160. Per il pensiero di Tertulliano sullo Spirito cfr. V. GROSSI, *Istituzione e Spirito in Tertulliano* (*De praescriptione – De pudicitia*), in "Augustinianum" 20 (1980), pp. 645-654.

are not different the one from the others, on the contrary they have a different function (*distributione*).[97]

The Spirit Holy for Tertullian is situated not to the third place in reason of the substance, but in the sense of the classification (gradus), that is to say in the way to present himself (form).[98] The true utterance consists for Tertullian in the unity of the divine persons and to the same time in the alterity of the same ones. It is also to say that the Spirit Holy for Tertullian is formed of a very thin matter that has the function, on the trace of the stoic spirit, to animate every thing.[99] Otherwise Origen will oppose himself to the material conception of the Spirit Holy. In fact Origen affirms in *Principles* 1,1,3 that "*the Spirit Holy is not able certainly to be understood as body*",[100] on the contrary "*it is intellectual substance and*

97 TERTULLIANO, *Contro Prassea* 9,2. Ed. crit. G. SCARPAT, *Q.S.F. Tertulliano. Contro Prassea*, p. 162.
98 TERTULLIANO, *Contro Prassea* 2,4. Ed. crit. G. SCARPAT, *Q.S.F. Tertulliano. Contro Prassea*, p. 146.
99 TERTULLIANO, *Il battesimo* 4,1. Ed. crit. R.F. REFOULÉ-M. DROUZY, *Tertullien. Traité du baptême*, Paris 1966, p. 69.
100 Ed. crit. H. CROUZEL-M. SIMONETTI, *Origène. Traité des principes,* p. 94. Trad. di M. SIMONETTI, *I Principi di Origine*, p. 129.

it has a proper subsistence".[101] In polemic against the modalists Origen affirms that the Spirit Holy is separated from the Father and from the Son and it is coeternal to God Father and to the Son.[102] Watered to the philosophical tendency middle-platonic Origen, although it affirms the coeternity of the Spirit Holy together with that one of the Father and of the Son and his personal distinction from that one of the Father and of the Son, it admits however the inferiority of rank of the Spirit in comparison with the Father and with the Son.[103]

4.2. The prefigurations of the Spirit Holy and prophetic inspiration

Origen in *Principles* 1,3 affirms that the Spirit Holy was prefigured by the Spirit of God who was on the waters, before the world was created. Another expression where Origen sees prefigured the Spirit Holy is "*the*

---

101 Ed. crit. H. CROUZEL-M. SIMONETTI, *Origène. Traité des principes,* p. 94. Trad. di M. SIMONETTI, *I Principi di Origene*, p. 130.

102 Cfr. M. SIMONETTI (a cura di), *I Principi di Origene*, p. 171.

103 Cfr. M. SIMONETTI (a cura di), *I Principi di Origene,* pp. 171-172.

spirit of the mouth of God" (Sal 32,6).[104] It is really a function of the Spirit Holy, for Origen, that one to sanctify the men that are worthy of it. Another text that Origen cites for showing that the Spirit Holy doesn't reside in the heart of whom is not worthy of to receive him it is Gen 6,3.[105] Also in Sal 103,29 is preannounced for Origen the action of the Spirit Holy who renews the earth, after having destroyed the sinners.[106] Also for Cyprian the Spirit Holy is the one who preannounces in image the future events.[107]

4.3. *The role of the Spirit in the incarnation*

́Tertullian not intends with the term Spirit only the third person of the trinity. Referring to Lc 1,35 why "*the Spirit Holy will come down on you and the potency of God it will shade you*" (Lc 1,35) Tertullian affirms in the *Flesh of Christ* 18,1.3, in polemic against the gnostics who denied the virginal birth of the Verb, that the Son of

---

104 M. SIMONETTI (a cura di), *I Principi di Origene,* p. 177.
105 Cfr. M. SIMONETTI (a cura di), *I Principi di Origene,* p. 175.
106 *Ibidem*
107 CIPRIANO, *Lettere* 63,4. Ed. crit. G.F. DIERCKS, *Sancti Cypriani episcopi. Epistularium*, Turnholti 1996, pp. 392-394.

God was born from the seed of God Father who is the Spirit.[108] Tertullian in the *Against Praxeas* 26,2.4 attribute an identity christological at the term Spirit. In fact for him the Spirit of God, through whom the Verb assumes the flesh in the breast of Mary, is the Verb of God or the Spirit of God who animates the Word.[109]

4.4. *The mission of the Spirit advocate*

Returning to Origen he affirms that the Spirit Holy is also denominated advocate because it teaches very greats truth, that not are comprehensible to the human intelligence.[110] Origen, full of platonic culture, it seems to refer to the myth of the cavern, where exactly Plato makes understand that the man during the terrestrial life it perceives the reflexes of the truth and, only when he draws near to the lamp of the truth, he can contemplate of

---

108 Ed. crit. J.P. MAHÉ, *Tertullien. La chair du Christ*, Paris 1975, p. 282-284. Trad. di C. MORESCHINI, *Opere scelte di Quinto Settimio Florente Tertulliano*, UTET, Torino 1974, pp. 759-760.
109 Ed. crit. G. SCARPAT, *Tertulliano. Contro Prassea*, Torino 1985, p. 221.
110 ORIGENE, *Principi* II,7,4. Ed. crit. H. CROUZEL-M. SIMONETTI, *Origène. Traité des principes*, Paris 1978, p. 332.

it the inexhaustible wealths that from it come. But if from a side Origen takes again the platonic motive of the search of the truth, that is light for the soul, from the other one it goes away for the fact that only the soul cannot reach the fullness of the truth, without the help of the Spirit Holy. In fact subsequently Origen affirms that the term advocate (paraclito) derives from consolation and, applied to the Spirit Holy, it comes to indicate that this is above all source of joyfullness and of consolation for those who are worthy to participate in his mysteries, through a progressive and internal spiritual knowledge.[111] It is present in Origen the ideal of the apathy ($\dot{\alpha}\pi\alpha\theta\epsilon\tilde{\iota}\alpha$) that in the greek thought, above all stoic, it was attainable with the only human strengths, while for Origene it is a divine gift of the Spirit. Origen adds that also Christ is denominated advocate (paraclito), because it intercedes for us near the Father for our sins and he underlines to the same time the double meaning of comforter with reference to Christ and to the Spirit.[112] Clement of

---

111 ORIGENE, *Principi* II,7,4. Ed. crit. H. CROUZEL-M. SIMONETTI, *Origène. Traité des principes*, Paris 1978, pp. 332-334.
112 ORIGENE, *Principi* II,7,4. Ed. crit. H. CROUZEL-M. SIMONETTI, *Origène. Traité des principes*, Paris 1978, p.

Alexandria, in particularly way, referring to the known motive protrepticus-Aristotelian of the knowledge of the truth[113], why the man was born, it applies such motive to the Spirit Holy. In fact he has been sent by God to make know to the men the truth that is the Word, the Verb of God. For Clement the truth is reached through the knowledge of the pity living in the alive faith and in the mutual love.[114] Clement of Alexandria therefore, referring to the 1Tm 2,4 and to the 1Tm 4,8, arrives at the conclusion that the one who practise the pity, her living with alive faith and in the free love, reaches the communion with Jesus Christus. The mission of the Advocate (paraclito) also in Tertullian it purchases a sense final. The Spirit Holy not only guides the believers in the truth in the present time, but it announces them the truth of Christ in the time last: he will come at the end of the times after the resurrection of the flesh to give the enjoyment of the celestial life to the saints, and to the

_____

334.
113 Cfr. G. LAZZATI, *L'Aristotele perduto e gli scrittori cristiani*, Vita e pensiero, Milano 1938.
114 Per l'argomento vedi GERARDO DI NOLA (ed.), *Lo Spirito Santo nella testimonianza dei Padri e degli Scrittori cristiani* (*I-V sec.*), Roma 1999, pp. 137-138.

wicked ones the punishments of the eternal fire.[115]

4.5. *The action of the Spirit in the baptismal water and in the baptism*

For Tertullian the Spirit Holy has the role of sanctifier of the waters of the baptism. Always for Tertullian he goes down from the sky, after the prayer of invocation, on the waters to make them holy.[116] Then Tertullian explains that the water sanctified by the Spirit; water that has received from the Spirit the ability to cure, it purifies not only the body but also the soul, whose the body is to service.[117] Tertullian affirms this one from the presupposition that any bodily element, that is situated under to a spiritual element that is composed of thin matter, it penetrates in the water so that, who dips oneself in the waters sanctified by the Spirit Holy, it goes out from there also him sanctified because his sins are

---

115 TERTULLIANO, *Sulla prescrizione contro gli eretici* 13,4. Ed. crit. R.F. REFOULÉ, *Quinti Septimi Florentis. Tertulliani Opera*, vol. I, Turnholti 1954, pp. 197-198.
116 TERTULLIANO, *Il battesimo* 4,4. Ed. crit. R.F. REFOULÉ-M. DROUZY, *Tertullien. Traité du baptême,* pp. 70-71.
117 TERTULLIANO, *Il battesimo* 4,5. Ed. crit. R.F. REFOULÉ-M. DROUZY, *Tertullien. Traité du baptême,* p. 71.

cancelled.[118] After having dealing with the action sanctifier of the water on behalf of the Spirit Holy, Tertullian describes the action sanctifier of the Spirit Holy in the man; action that is revealed in the unction and in the imposition of the hands.[119] For Tertullian the Spirit goes down on the baptized man. This descent of the Spirit on the baptized one, that also for Clement it is consequent to the remission of the sins, it is named illumination. With this image Clement of Alexandria wants to affirm that only the eye of the spirit of the man, free from the sins and similar to the light (φωτεινόν), it can see the descent of the Spirit Holy on the baptized one.[120] This mission of the Spirit, returning to Tertullian, it also has an effect divine and anthropological: the baptized one in the baptism arrives at the resemblance of God; resemblance that had been lost with the original

118 TERTULLIANO, *Il battesimo* 4,1.7,2. Ed. crit. R.F. REFOULÉ-M. DROUZY, *Tertullien. Traité du baptême,* pp. 69.76.
119 TERTULLIANO, *Il battesimo* 7,1-2.8,1-2. Ed. crit. R.F. REFOULÉ-M. DROUZY, *Tertullien. Traité du baptême,* pp. 76-77.
120 CLEMENTE ALESSANDRINO, *Pedagogo* I,6,26,1-2.28,1. Ed. crit. H.I. MARROU-M. HARL, *Clément d'Alexandrie. Le Pédagogue*, Paris 1960, pp. 158-162.

sin.[121]

4.6. *The church is the place of the Spirit*

The unity of the church for Cyprian sinks its roots in Christ, unique head and in the living action of his Spirit.[122] Consequently Cyprian adds that out of the church it is not possible to receive neither the Spirit Holy, neither the remission of the sins.[123] Also for Tertullian the church is the place of the Spirit because the Spirit, since teacher of truth, has been sent in the world by the Father and he has the assignment to conduct the church to the truth.[124]

---

121 TERTULLIANO, *Il battesimo* 5,7. Ed. crit. R.F. REFOULÉ-M. DROUZY, *Tertullien. Traité du baptême,* p. 74.
122 CIPRIANO, *L'unità della chiesa cattolica* 5. Ed. crit. P. SINISCALCO-P. MATTEI-M. POIRIER, *Cyprien de Carthage. L'unité de l'Église*, Paris 2006, pp. 182-186. Vedi anche TERTULLIANO, *La prescrizione contro gli eretici* 20. Ed. crit. R.F. REFOULÉ, *Quinti Septimi Florentis. Tertulliani Opera*, pp. 201-202.
123 CIPRIANO, *Lettere* 73,6-7. Ed. crit. Vedi sulla teologia dello Spirito dopo Tertulliano M. SIMONETTI, *Il regresso della teologia dello Spirito Santo in Occidente dopo Tertulliano*, in "Augustinianum" 20 (1980), pp. 655-669.
124 TERTULLIANO, *La prescrizione contro gli eretici* 28. Ed. crit. R.F. REFOULÉ, *Quinti Septimi Florentis. Tertulliani Opera,* p. 209.

5. THE HEURISTIC ASPECTS OF THE FUNCTION AND OF THE IDENTITY OF THE SPIRIT IN THE FATHERS CAPPADOCIAN: THE IDENTITY OF THE SPIRIT HOLY IN THE IMMANENT TRINITY

5.1. *The Spirit Holy is not a creature*

For Fathers Cappadocian one intend the Fathers that have contributed to give a notable impulse to the doctrinal elaboration of the pneumatic theology, in a period in which were spread the heresy of Eunomius and that one on the Spirit. Eunomius sustained that the Spirit Holy was a creature of the Son, who in turn was creature of the Father, because for him only the Father was not generated (*ἀγέννητος*). The pneumatomachoi placed the Spirit between God and the creatures. Basil, to defend the patrimony of the faith from the attacks of Eunomius, affirms in *The against Eunomius* III,1-6 that the Spirit Holy is not a creature, because also the testimonies transmitted in the Writings show that the Spirit has a nature, that is above that one of the creatures. Basil specifies that the Spirit Holy is not of different nature from that one of the Father and of the Son, as Eunomius sustained, even if a difference of order and of dignity exists among the Father, the Son and the Spirit.[125] Basil, countering to Eunomius that the Spirit is not of different nature from that one of the Father and of the Son, rejects the diakonia of the Spirit. This concept of diakonia from Tatian was transmitted along the centuries until Basil, who banishes it entirely.[126]

5.2. *The Spirit Holy is God*

The merit of Gregory Nazianzen has been that one to have affirmed that the Spirit Holy is God.[127] Before him Basil had not expressly affirmed that the Spirit Holy is God, because according to him this truth was not contained in the Writings. Nevertheless Basil believed that the Spirit Holy was worthy of the same honor and adoration that was bestowed to God Father, because it

---

125 Cfr. GERARDO DI NOLA (ed.), *Lo Spirito Santo nella testimonianza dei Padri e degli Scrittori cristiani* (*I-V sec.*), Roma 1999, pp. 474-475.
126 BASILIO, *Contro Eunomio* 3,1-2. Ed. crit. B. SESBOUÉ-G.M. DE DURAND-L. DOUTRELEAU, *Basile de Césarée. Contre Eunome*, Paris 1983, pp. 144-154.
127 GREGORIO DI NAZIANZO, *Discorsi teologici* 31,3.6. Ed. crit. P. GALLAY, *Grégoire de Nazianze, Discours 27-31*, Paris 1978, pp. 278-280.284-286.

was not of different nature from that one of the Father but it had "relationship with the Father and the Son".[128] Gregory Nazianzen, specifying that the Spirit Holy is God, it underlines that the element hypostatic of the Spirit, that is to say what founds his individuality is the idea of the relation of origin.[129] As the Father has one his property hypostatic, because he is not generated and as the Son has also him another property hypostatic because he has been generated by the Father; equally the Spirit Holy, always for Gregory Nazianzen, it has an own reality hypostatic that comes him from the relation of origin or better from the understood procession in immanent sense. In fact for Gregory Nazianzen the Spirit Holy assumes an own individuality, because it is the one who proceeds without having been generated.[130] Basil,

---

128 BASILIO, *Contro Eunomio* 3,3. Ed. crit. B. SESBOUÉ-G.M. DE DURAND- L. DOUTRELEAU, *Basile de Césarée. Contre Eunome*, pp. 154-156. Trad. di GERARDO DI NOLA (ed.), *Lo Spirito Santo nella testimonianza dei Padri e degli Scrittori cristiani* (*I-V sec.*), p. 476.
129 GREGORIO DI NAZIANZO, *Discorsi teologici* 31,9. Ed. crit. P. GALLAY, *Grégoire de Nazianze, Discours 27-31*, pp. 290-292.
130 GREGORIO DI NAZIANZO, *Discorsi teologici* 30,19. Ed. crit. P. GALLAY, *Grégoire de Nazianze, Discours 27-31*, pp. 264-266.

instead, to define the property hypostatic of the Spirit Holy, it recurs to the attribute of the holiness that doesn't implicate the relation of origin, because for Basil the Spirit Holy not draws the own origin from the procession. For him the identity hypostatic of the Spirit Holy makes itself manifest in the name.[131]

5.3. *The Spirit Holy is consubstantial with the Father and the Son*

Gregory of Nyssa, brother of Basil, has had the great merit to specify which role occupies the Son in the procession of the Spirit, ever since Basil was limited oneself to underline the coming out of the Spirit from the Father. Gregory of Nyssa detains himself on this point and he sustains that the Spirit not only goes out (ἐκπορεύεται) of the Father (ἐκ τοῦ πατρός) but through the Son (διά τοῦ υἱοῦ) and, as such, the Son comes to be the middleman between the Father and the Spirit.[132] For

131 BASILIO, *Contro Eunomio* III,2-4. Ed. crit. B. SESBOUÉ-G.M. DE DURAND-L. DOUTRELEAU, *Basile de Césarée. Contre Eunome*, pp. 153-163.
132 GREGORIO DI NISSA, *Non sono tre dei.* Ed. crit. J.P. MIGNE, *Patrologiae. Cursus completus*, vol. 45, Parisiis 1863, col. 125B. Per l'argomento vedi GERARDO DI NOLA (ed.), *Lo Spirito Santo nella testimonianza dei Padri e degli Scrittori*

Gregory of Nyssa, therefore, as the Son receives the being from the Father because it is from him generated, equally the Spirit, who becomes the caused one, receives the being from the Father who is the cause of it through the Son.[133] Gregory of Nyssa to such intention uses the image of the lamp, to make understand that as the lamp transmits his own light to another and, through this to a third, equally the Spirit Holy proceeds from the same and only person of God Father, from whom also the Son has been generated and through whom the Spirit receives the being from the Father.[134]

---

cristiani (I-V sec.), pp. 539-540.
133 GREGORIO DI NISSA, Non sono tre dei. Ed. crit. J.P. MIGNE, Patrologiae. Cursus completus, vol. 45, col. 133B.
134 GREGORIO DI NISSA, Contro i macedoniani 13. Ed. crit. J.P. MIGNE, Patrologiae. Cursus completus, vol. 45, col. 1316-1317. In generale sulla figura di Gregorio di Nissa vedi C. MORESCHINI, Opere di Gregorio di Nissa, Torino 1992.

Conclusion

In this search we have had the opportunity to point out, from the reading of the sources and of the relative specific studies both to monographic character and not, the most meaningful lines on the reality of the Spirit Holy in the Fathers of the church in an arc of time that goes from the I to the IV sec. d.C. We have undertaken the search from the Apostolic Fathers, where we have had the opportunity to ascertain that the doctrine of the Spirit Holy is about similar to that one taught in the Gospel. In them one reflect the life of the first christian communities where it is preponderant the faith in the Spirit, besides that one in God Father and in Jesus. We are well distant from a rational formulation on the Spirit, that will have instead its beginning with the apologists. In fact all what the Apostolic Fathers tell with regard to the Spirit it is not formulated, as says S. Priest "as made the gnostics in the forms reduced and oblique of rational concepts",[1] there it is on the contrary in the Fathers the genuine sense of a faith lived in the Spirit that

---

1 S. PRETE, *In incorruptibilitate*, p. 521.

is made know, according to their creed, both in vertical sense and horizontal. In vertical sense their faith is established more on the divinity of the Spirit that not on the Son's distinction from the Spirit. The Spirit becomes besides for them source of prophetic inspiration and author of the messianic prophecies that are realized in Jesus. In horizontal sense the Spirit Holy is the author of the effusion of the charismas in the church and to him it is conferred the power to sanctify the souls. If from a part with the pologists we be somehow in line of continuity with the Apostolic Fathers, above all in the horizontal sense concerning the action of the Spirit in the church, in the vertical sense however it is begun to make a first rational reflection, using philosophical data to arrive to speak more of the logos that not of the Spirit, because the apologists have not proposed further elements to specify the distinction of the Spirit from the Verb. In concomitance with the Apostolic Fathers the apologists confess the divinity of the Verb and of the Spirit. With Irenaeus the datum revealed of the Spirit is developed more in the field of the trinity economic that in that one of the immanent trinity: the verb and the wisdom are the two hands with whom God creates the world. The verb, with his carnal birth, not only it has revealed the Father but it is become pawn of salvation for those who have believed in him. The Spirit Holy, in continuity with the Apostolic Fathers and with the Father apologists, has also for Irenaeus the supernatural role to sanctify the souls to conduct her to God. He has also been in old Testament the inspirer of the messianic prophecies. The merit of Tertullian has been that one to affirm the with-substance of the Spirit with that one of the Father in the distinction of the hypostasis, and therefore the personality of the Spirit. This to fight the conception of the heretical gnosis that reduced the three divine persons, included the Spirit to the triple show of an only person who is that one of the Father. Origen, to fight the heresy of Sabellius, defends the personality of the Spirit Holy denominating her "intellectual hypostasis" even if, in his doctrine of the Spirit, it considers the Spirit Holy an inferior person to that one of God and of the Son. In Clement of Alexandria it is preponderant the role of the Spirit sanctifier in the baptism and in the spirit of the men, while Cyprian not brings any element of novelty to his theology of the Spirit. Even if we have seen a certain doctrinal development in Origen and in Tertullian, there is to say that it is above all with the Fathers Cappadocian that we have had a real copernican revolution with regard to the datum revealed of the Spirit Holy. These ones, referring themselves to the thought of Origen, not only refuse the inferiority of nature of the Spirit, reestablishing the full affiliation of the Spirit to the divine triad, but they have deduced the character hypostatic of the Spirit both from the holiness and from the relation of origin that does of him the Spirit of the Father and of the Son. In few words the Fathers Cappadocian have had the ability to give an organic account of the bases of the faith on the revelation of the Spirit Holy, definitely defeating the heresy of Sabellius, that one of Eunomius and that one of Macedonius (pneumatomachian).

BIBLIOGRAFIA ESSENZIALE

FONTI:

BARCELLONA F.S (a c. di), *Epistola di Barnaba,* Torino 1975.

BURINI C. (a cura di), *Gli Apologeti greci*, Roma 1986.

CROUZEL H. -M. SIMONETTI, *Origène. Traité des principes,* Paris 1978.

DATTRINO L. (a cura di), *Gerardo di Nola. Lo Spirito Santo nella testimonianza dei Padri e degli scrittori cristiani (I-V sec.),* Roma 1999.

DIERCKS G.F., *Sancti Cypriani episcopi. Epistularium,* Turnholti 1996.

GALLAY P. (a cura di), *Grégoire de Nazianze, Discours 27-31*, Paris 1978.

GRAMAGLIA P. (a cura di), *Atenagora, Supplica per i cristiani*, Torino 1964.

GRAMAGLIA P. (a cura di), *Tertulliano. Il battesimo,* Roma 1979.

JOLY R. (a cura di), *Hermas, Le Pasteur,* Paris 1958.

MAHÉ J.P., *Tertullien. La chair du Christ,* Paris 1975.

MARROU H.I. -HARL M., *Clément d'Alexandrie. Le Pédagogue*, Paris 1960.

MIGLIORE F. (a cura di), *Clemente Alessandrino. Protrettico ai greci,* Roma 2004.

MIGNE J.P. (ed.), *Patrologiae. Cursus completus,* vol. 45, Paris 1863.

MORESCHINI C. (a cura di), *Opere di Gregorio di Nissa,* UTET, Torino 1992.

MORESCHINI C. (a cura di), *Opere scelte di Quinto Settimio Florente Tertulliano,* UTET, Torino 1974.

NORELLI E. (a cura di), *A Diogneto*, Milano 1991.

PERETTO E. (a cura di), *Epideixis. Antico catechismo degli adulti,* Roma 1981.

PINI G. (a cura di), *Clemente Alessandrino, Gli Stromati. Note di vera filosofia*, Milano 1985

QUACQUARELLI A. (a cura di), *I Padri Apostolici,* Roma 1998.

RACCONE A.R. (a cura di), *San Giustino. Le due Apologie,* Roma 1983.

REFOULÉ R.F., *Quinti Septimi Florentis. Tertulliani Opera*, vol. I, Turnholti 1954.

REFOULÉ R.F. -DROUZY M., *Tertullien. Traité du baptême*, Paris 1966.

ROUSSEAU A.-DOUTRELEAU L.-MERCIER Ch., *Irénée de Lyon. Contre les hérésies I-V*, Paris 1969-1979.

SCARPAT G. (a cura di), *Q.S.F. Tertulliano, Contro Prassea*, Torino 1985.

SESBOUÉ B. DE DURAND S-G.M.-DOUTRELEAU L., *Basile de Césarée. Contre Eunome*, Paris 1983.

SIMONETTI M. (a cura di), *I Principi di Origene*, Torino 1968.

SINISCALCO P.-MATTEI P.-POIRIER M., *Cyprien de Carthage. L'unité de l'Église*, Paris 2006.

TESSORE D., *Clemente Alessandrino. Il Pedagogo*, Roma 2005.

VISONÁ G. (a cura di), *S. Giustino, Dialogo con Trifone*, Milano 1988.

XAVER FUNK F.-BIHLMEYER K.-WHITTAKER M., *Die Apostolischen Väter. Griechisch-deutsche Parallelausgabe*, Tübingen 1992.

STUDI:

BOLGIANI F., *Διακονία τοῦ πνεύματος* - *Fortuna e sfortuna di una formula teologica,* in "Augustinianum" 20 (1980), pp. 523-543.

CONGAR Y., *Credo nello Spirito Santo,* vol. I. *Rivelazione e esperienze dello spirito,* vol. III. *Teologia dello Spirito Santo,* Brescia 1984.1987.

FELICI S. (a cura di), *Spirito Santo e catechesi patristica,* Roma 1983.

GERVAIS A., *Les missions divines de St. Justin à Origène,* Fribourg 1958.

GROSSI V., *Istituzione e Spirito in Tertulliano (De praescriptione - De pudicitia),* in "Augustinianum" 20 (1980), pp. 645-654.

LEBRETON J., *Histoire du dogme de la Trinité,* voll. I-II, Paris 1927-28.

MARTIN J.P., *Il rapporto tra Pneuma ed Ecclesia nella letteratura dei primi secoli cristiani,* in "Augustinianum" 20 (1980), pp. 471-483.

MESSANA V., *Lo Spirito santo e l'accezione Clementina di senso spirituale,* in "Augustinianum"

20 (1980), pp. 485-497.

MONACI CASTAGNO A. (a cura di), *Origene, Dizionario, la cultura, il pensiero, le opere*, Roma 2000.

MORESCHINI C., *Tradizione e innovazione nella pneumatologia di Tertulliano*, in "Augustinianum" 20 (1980), pp. 633-644.

PERETTO E., *La Epideixis di Ireneo. Il ruolo dello Spirito nella formulazione delle argomentazioni*, in "Augustinianum" 20 (1980), pp. 559-579.

PRETE S., *In incorruptibilitate (ἀφθαρσία) Spiritus s. (Mart. Polyc. 14,2)*, in "Augustinianum" 20 (1980), pp. 509-521.

RIGGI C., *Lo Spirito Santo nell'antropologia della I Clementis*, in "Augustinianum" 20 (1980), pp. 499-507.

RORDORF W., *"Qui natus est de Spiritu sancto et Maria Virgine*, in "Augustinianum" 20 (1980), pp. 545-557.

SIMONETTI M., *Il regresso della teologia dello Spirito Santo in Occidente dopo Tertulliano*, in "Augustinianum" 20 (1980), pp. 655-669.

ALTRI SCRITTI CONSULTATI:

BOLGIANI F., *Spirito Santo* in A. Di BERARDINO (a cura di), *Dizionario patristico e di antichità cristiane*, vol. II, Casale Monferrato 1983, col. 3285-3298.

BOSIO C.-DAL COVOLO E., -MARITANO M., *Introduzione ai Padri della chiesa sec. I-II; II-III e III-IV,* voll. 3, Torino 1990-1991.1993.

CASAMASSA P.A., *Gli Apologisti greci. Studio introduttivo*, Roma 1944.

DANIÉLOU J., *Origène, La table ronde*, Paris 1948.

GIRGENTI G., *Giustino martire. Il primo cristiano platonico. Con in appendice "Atti del martirio di San Giustino"*, Milano 1995.

LAZZATI G., *L'Aristotele perduto e gli scrittori cristiani,* Milano 1938.

LILLA S., *Introduzione al medioplatonismo,* Roma 1992.

MORESCHINI C.-NORELLI E., *Storia della letteratura cristiana antica greca e latina,* voll. I-II, Brescia 1996.

ORBE A., *La teologia dei secoli II-III, il confronto della grande chiesa con lo gnosticismo,* Roma 1995.

PARENTE M.I. (a cura di), *Stoici antichi*, voll. I-II, Torino 1989.

QUASTEN J., *Patrologia*, voll. I-II, Casale 1983.

SIMONETTI M., *Origene esegeta e la sua tradizione*, Brescia 2004.

SPANNEUT M., *Le stoicisme des Pères de l'Église de Clement de Rome a Clément d'Alexandrie*, Paris 1957.

youcanprint

Finito di stampare nel mese di Gennaio 2016
per conto di Youcanprint *Self-Publishing*